Guided Meditation

Learn Mindfulness and Fall Asleep Faster

(Improve Positive Thinking-quiet Your Mind for a Better Life)

Cynthia Baker

Published By **Phil Dawson**

Cynthia Baker

All Rights Reserved

Guided Meditation: Learn Mindfulness and Fall Asleep Faster (Improve Positive Thinking-quiet Your Mind for a Better Life)

ISBN 978-1-77485-975-9

No part of this guidebook shall be reproduced in any form without permission in writing from the publisher except in the case of brief quotations embodied in critical articles or reviews.

Legal & Disclaimer

The information contained in this ebook is not designed to replace or take the place of any form of medicine or professional medical advice. The information in this ebook has been provided for educational & entertainment purposes only.

The information contained in this book has been compiled from sources deemed reliable, and it is accurate to the best of the Author's knowledge; however, the Author cannot guarantee its accuracy and validity and cannot be held liable for any errors or omissions. Changes are periodically made to this book. You must consult your doctor or get professional medical advice before using any of the suggested remedies, techniques, or information in this book.

Upon using the information contained in this book, you agree to hold harmless the Author from and against any damages, costs, and expenses, including any legal fees potentially resulting from the application of any of the information provided by this guide. This disclaimer applies to any damages or injury caused by the use and application, whether directly or indirectly, of any advice or information presented, whether for breach of contract, tort, negligence, personal injury, criminal intent, or under any other cause of action.

You agree to accept all risks of using the information presented inside this book. You need to consult a professional medical practitioner in order to ensure you are both able and healthy enough to participate in this program.

Table of contents

Chapter 1: Preparing Yourself For Good Sleep 1

Chapter 2: Breathing Is Life 27

Chapter 3: Let Us Meditate On Meditation . 55

Chapter 4: How To Cultivate Inner Balance In A World Always In Hurry. Personal Growth, Respect, Awareness, Self-Esteem 87

Chapter 5: Does Fasting Make You More Able To Meditate Well? 105

Chapter 6: Mantras, What They Are, How They Can Be Used, Why They Are Important 111

Chapter 7: The Correct Position For The Hands In Meditation 131

Chapter 8: Transcendental Meditating: Techniques, Origins & Benefits 142

Chapter 1: Preparing Yourself For Good Sleep
Here we are, please.

You are now in a safe spot; everything will be alright.

As an opening chapter, I want to allow space for sleep. To rest. To sleep is the purest, simplest, and most natural state of being.

Good rest is essential for our bodies and minds to function properly throughout the day. Sleep is good for your body and helps you stay healthy.

Sleep does a fundamental job of cleaning out the brain. This allows us to avoid overloading it with the flood of information we have accumulated over the course of the day. When we are asleep, our memories are transferred from one day to the next. Also, synapses and brain connections are rearranged. All this is for the benefit to learning processes. Sleep improves memory, consolidates memories, and makes it possible to access new information. This is why, after a hard night's sleep, it is difficult to focus and makes it impossible for us to store any new information.

Sleep improves our quality of life and is good for the heart. Good sleep at night is great for our well-being, especially if it is consistent and uninterrupted.

Sleeping poorly can impact certain aspects of your life. It can even lead to stress that can become chronic or acute. A constant fatigue can cause memory problems, and even make it harder to make decisions. An insufficient amount of sleep causes a reduction in the energy reserve of the blood and muscles, leading to fatigue.

Before we get started with the sleep induction, I would like to ask for your kindnesses. Please put your phone away and mute the ringtone.

Avoid televisions and digital screens. Blue light has been shown by studies to lower the sleep-inducing hormone Melatonin.

Turn off the lights.

If it pleases you, you might keep a low light on. This could be the one that is on the table beside the bed or a scented candles that releases a relaxing aroma.

You can leave all the sound out of the room.

Do not allow anyone to interrupt or disturb this moment.

As the protagonist, you are the only one who matters. The focus is on you and your inner balance.

Now, put yourself in a relaxed place.

Do not allow any weight to be placed on your arms or legs.

Wearing tight clothing on your feet or shoes will cause you to feel uncomfortable.

Before you step out for the night, ensure that you have done your entire night's routine.

Be kind and say goodbye to everyone.

Make sure to stop at the restroom to brush your teeth.

It is best to plan ahead for everything, including clean clothes, shoes, colors, and materials.

Being prepared for the next day is an important first step to combat anxiety. While it all depends on our individual personalities, being organized is a good first step to counter anxiety. However, the effort is minimal and the rewards are significant. Do not be afraid of being late. Avoid starting your day with stress and the pressure of trying to finish everything quickly.

Once we're ready, we can learn a proven and widely used method to stop negative thoughts and induce sleep in a relaxing and refreshing way.

The technique works by regulating the breathing rhythm using numbers. In practice, the amount of oxygen in the body will have a calming effect on your nervous system. Although it may not initially seem to work well, it will over time have surprising results.

It is simple to use so it can be used anywhere.

Halt! Do not hold your breath! It's best to learn the technique, then practice breathing again when you aren't pregnant.

Gently place your tip of the tongue against the tissue behind your upper incisors.

Close your eyes.

Let's just relax.

Everything is good.

First, take a deep breathe and exhale as much air out as possible.

Breathe into your mouth, creating a sound similar in tone to a slight rustle.

With your mouth closed, exhale through you nose, and mentally count to 4.

One, two and three...

Now, hold your breathe for seven seconds. It's as if the water is boiling in your mouth.

One two three five six seven

For eight count, inhale deeply through your mouth.

One... Two... Three... Four... Five... Six Seven Eight ...

Good.

Now, we slowly repeat it.

Breathe through your mouth and make a sound that sounds like a slight buzz. You might also imagine blowing out the candles on a birthday cake.

Close your mouth, exhale through you nose, and mentally count up to four.

One two three four...

Hold your breath for seven benefits seconds.

One two three five six seven

Now exhale completely and count up to eight.

One... Two... Three... Four... Fifteen... Six... Seven Eight ...

You are doing amazing.

Last time, we are.

Breathe in with your mouth and produce a sound like a slight "rustle". This time, think of the paper creaking, or of a page being flipped.

You can clench your lips, inhale through you nose and count silently to four.

One two three four...

You can hold your breath for seven seconds.

One two three five six seven

Next, inhale through your mouth fully as you count up to eight.

One... Two... Three... Four... Five... Six... Seven Eight ...

You should now feel more relaxed, calm and at peace.

This exercise can be repeated at any hour of your day, as I have mentioned. Let me tell you a story. You need to go to work, or you have an appointment up on the roof. In this case, instead of climbing stairs, you can use an elevator. This is a great way to relax and focus instead of looking at people or checking in the mirror. This may not be the best setting because the air in small spaces often is very saturated and full with bacteria. However, it can be a good practice if you don't have enough time to look at other people or go outside for four steps. It's not worth it!

If this is any consolation for you, it is because insomnia affects many people. Millions of people across all ages, races, and backgrounds report sleeping disorders every year. Many of these sleep disorders are caused by stress that is increased by fatigue or reduced mental lucidity.

Let's find out what suggestions I have to offer to combat insomnia and anxiety about not sleeping, which can cause more stress and anxiety.

First of all, I have some good news for you right now. Insomnia can be caused by bad habits or pathological conditions, but not in all cases.

This means that effective behavioral countermeasures are possible to intervene.

Three scenarios are possible for someone to say they have trouble sleeping:

When he can't sleep, when sleep isn't continuous and there are frequent wake-ups, or when you wake too early to go to sleep.

The fear of not being capable of sleeping is one the most common modern phobias.

Restorative rest isn't just a word. An adequate amount of sleep at night can have direct and indirect effects on the health of your body and should not ever be sacrificed.

It's well known that those with the best physical and athletic abilities are the greatest champions in sport. They sleep an average of twelve hours per day. All the benefits can be activated by this method.

Being able to reach the end of the day without feeling like a mass of nerves is a good way to fall asleep when it is bedtime.

Truth be told, eliminating stimulants from the body by mid-day would be the best option.

I say you should quit drinking after lunch.

Avoid any stimuli, let's say neurological, after dinner. You shouldn't do activities at high intensity or very loud noises in the evening.

While it may seem strange that people fall asleep while watching TV, many others do. While they might fall asleep after work, it is possible that they are tired. On the other hand, the TV can wake them up if the volume changes. In any event, sleep quality may be compromised.

It is possible that this could alter your dreams or moods. You may be captivated by a thriller film that is suspenseful, but it can also trigger emotions which can impact your peace of Mind.

This is what I love to emphasize: although man is adaptable, it has evolved over millions of year. This means that the two hundred years of artificial lighting, as well as TV background noises, have been equivalent to the blinking of an eye.

It is not true that we are well-suited to staying up late like predators. The night is quiet, dark and frightening for humans. We don't have the organs or sense of smell to guide us in low-light situations. Even though we are a strong evolutionary force, we haven't gone so far as dominating the night. Although it is normal to remain awake long after sunset due to artificial lighting, we are taking away space that would be necessary for a well-deserved and essential rest.

Our circadian rhythms, which are tuned to the day-night cycle, are set to produce physiological changes that prepare us not only to wake up, but also to go to sleep. You should not hinder the "sleepiness", which is essential for good sleep.

Relaxation after dinner is the best activity.

Dimming the lights in the home is a good way to emulate the sunset's phases, which begin at dusk. A light that gradually dims from dawn to the time the sun disappears behind it. The blinds are available in the house. You can also close the shutters or frames of the window frames.

You should set the TV to an acceptable volume if it is your intention to watch. To attract viewers' attention, many of the new productions use acoustic shocked. A TV program's commercials often break in at a louder volume than normal.

Another option, which I highly recommend, if you are suffering from sleep problems and have trouble falling asleep, is to listen to low-volume, non-invasive music, take a herbal tea and read a good book.

Don't go to bed too late if you can. Consider when to go to bed. You may think that people who go to bed later than others are old or mature. However, as you get older and realize how busy your schedule becomes, the amount of sleep you need is not enough to replace the youthful vigor.

We are all more aware of the importance and value of sleep as we age. However, in situations where we do not sleep well or suffer from constant insomnia, we must face another fear: the fear of losing our sleep.

This is often why a person chooses to go to sleep early, sometimes unconsciously.

However, it is possible to fall asleep on your couch while the TV is turned up loud. You wake up more tired at night than ever and can't get a good night's sleep.

This is why it's best to get to sleep immediately after waking up and not care about the "aging look". It makes no sense.

People who have trouble sleeping at night may find it helpful to take a so-called power nap, which is an Anglo-Saxon term and much more fashionable than the "nap".

This can often manifest as post-prandial insomnia, which is due to a more complex digestion. When you eat a lot of carbs at lunchtime, it can lead to drowsiness, particularly if you need to work in afternoon.

The power nap can be used to recharge batteries for up to twenty minutes. This is so that you don't have to disrupt your sleep at night.

You may find it useful to take a break in the afternoon when your working, managerial, and parent conditions permit.

Sleeping is essential for good health. It is generally accepted that sleep is good for you.

We are blessed to live in an age that recognizes the science of sleep and has developed technology to help us improve quality through improved environments and better tools.

We don't sleep on uncomfortable beds anymore. The home environment today is less hostile than in the past. It's possible to wear warm but lightweight clothing while you sleep. You can also set the temperature to a cooler setting. You can adjust the room's brightness to make it darker. Additionally, you can isolate a space acoustically in order to block outside noise.

It is important to choose the best position for you, and I say that often. Do not fall asleep in uncomfortable positions that cause you to wake up every morning. In terms of bedroom design, be mindful of functionality. Not fashion.

There may be a number of factors that can cause you to feel tired, exhausted, and lazy mentally. You need to plan your day in such a way that it allows you to rest for a few moments after each of the tasks on the schedule.

You can't live without rest and sleep!

It is, in fact, a key weapon to feeling good and having a fulfilling life.

Sleep is fundamental for psychophysical recovery. It is important for cell repair, cell regeneration, and for the repair or damage that builds up day by day. However, it is very clear that when sleep is not sufficient, it makes it difficult to live a happy, fulfilled life. Sleepiness and anpathy go hand-in-hand.

Some forms of insomnia can be caused externally by factors like an addictive substance abuse problem or a hostile sleep environment. It is possible to address the problem by changing the external factor. In cases of "primary sleeplessness", which is not due to secondary causes, a vicious circle can develop where you feel angry and frustrated at the inability to sleep. In such cases, it is vital to end the cycle.

Let us continue our journey.

Below are three strategies that I have found to be effective in randomized controlled trials.

Stop complaining about sleep. Our collective agreement is that chronic insomnia can be extremely frustrating. People who live in fear every night, wake up at the crack of dawn and stare at the clock until it's time for them to rise, start developing negative emotions such anxiety, fear, fear and anger as a result of trying to fall asleep. Stimulus therapy is designed to break this link and make it clear that sleep is only associated with the bed. This is a recommendation from doctors. If you truly cannot sleep, it may be advisable to turn off your alarm clock and put your bed in another room.

If you can't sleep, don't lie down in bed trying to fall asleep. If you have tried to fall asleep for more then twenty-three minutes, it is time to get up and move on. Try to pee or to read something light. Take a walk towards the living room and don't use the computer, telephone, or television. You should also avoid eating nighttime snacks that could be used as fuel for the fire. Experts agree that getting out the bed when you're not sleeping is an effective way to end the cycle of negative emotions associated with the bed. However, it must be done properly. Also, sweet sleep deprivation can make it easier to go to sleep the next day.

This means that instead of worrying about how bad your morning will be because you're tired, you can think this will help you sleep better at night.

There are always two sides of a coin!

A second strategy is relaxation. Relaxation should be practiced and surrounded with relaxing elements. Stress hormones are produced when anxiety makes it hard to sleep. It can be helpful to practice relaxation. As we discussed at the start of this story and will continue to see, there are a variety of techniques for progressive muscle relax (focusing on relaxing each section of the body in its own sequence) or meditation via controlled breathing.

This is the last strategy that was demonstrated: Change your thinking about sleep. People who feel stressed out about not being able to sleep well tend to exaggerate the problem. They may believe they slept less, which is a common mistake. These negative thoughts are a way to reduce stress. It is possible to create a relaxing environment such as a dark and quiet room that encourages sleep.

There are some tips that aren't scientifically valid but work for insomnia sufferers of all types.

First, the advice not to try too hard. As absurd as it may sound, falling asleep might be as simple as trying to stay awake. Insomniacs tend to fall asleep faster if they're happy to be awake, and less worried about falling asleep. Statistically, this is because you can forget about looking at your phone, computer, or any other device, and instead just do nothing. You remove anxiety from trying to fall asleep.

There are activities that will help you manage night anxiety and also address the root causes.

The first is physical activity. It is important to move in order to reduce anxiety, especially night anxiety. You will arrive at bed more relaxed and physically exhausted, which will make it easier to fall asleep.

If anxiety occurs in the evening, such as when there is boredom or isolation, you can combat night anxiety by changing the way you organize your evenings and seeking more opportunities to socialize. Have any other ideas? There are many options. A dance class, a film festival at the home once a fortnight, inviting friends, some dinners at home or out, with or without friends. You can also do solo activities such as reading a good funny book.

You can finally put an end to cigarettes and alcohol. Although some people may not be addicted to cigarettes or alcohol, others are. It is important to recognize that alcohol can interfere with mental activity and affect sleep health. Cigarettes stimulate synaptic activities and are a vasoconstrictor. It alters normal brain microcirculation. You should stop smoking or drinking alcohol in the evenings. It is important to establish a healthy rhythm that not only affects your daily activities, but also your body. This will help you sleep well and relieve anxiety.

Do me a big and noticeable favor by not constantly rewinding the same thoughts.

Anxiety can often be a result of too many unfounded, sometimes exaggerated worries. Talk to someone who will listen and vent your worries. At least once a week, sit down and open your bag with a friend, family member, professional, or trusted individual.

Sometimes, all that is needed to remove unnecessary stress and anxiety from your life is to consider another perspective.

Remember, breathing is the best medicine we have, but it is not often remembered. It is possible to get back your best faculties by learning to breathe well. Not only to increase oxygenation, but also to "relax" from anxiety and calm down the negative thoughts that can distract us from our potential.

"The heart acts on the breath" is the meaning of this expression. The only door that allows the body to act on an unvoluntary function, like the heart, is the breath. The heart's motion affects the air, so the breath that helps you control the most inappropriate emotions is also affected.

Breathing is also the very first act we do when we enter this world. It is the primordial action that marks the beginning of our journey into life. Ancient wisdom holds that the soul that was given to us at birth is returned when we breathe our last, on the point where death is reached. This primordial exchange is between us and the universe.

Most of the time, we breathe without realizing that it is happening. It is therefore important to regain some sense of awareness about one's breathing.

The breathing rate is the amount of breaths taken per minute. It includes an inhalation, an expiratory phase, and the pause that separates them form the single respiratory cycle.

There are times when it becomes difficult to breathe. At these times, we often use our mouths instead of our nose.

The nose filters air and plays an important immunological role. However, in the most intense times of life we breath with the mouth. This also happens at death when we check for the air that is clinging onto every breath. Notice when you aren't breathing.

It is not uncommon to forget to breath in tension situations and stay suspended.

Use breathing to manage your emotions. This is a powerful skill that everyone has and will always possess, no matter where they are located.

How we feel affects how our breathing changes. Our emotions are also reflected in the way that our breath vibrates. In dangerous situations, the heartbeat can accelerate and the respiratory rate will increase. Although it can be hard to manage fear, it has a basic biological function and protects us. The problem is that we are programmed for stress relief, even if they become a daily routine.

You feel like you are in a drowning situation. Anguish and anxiety can become chasms that cannot be escaped, and your heart explodes. You can't just repeat that all is well. It is difficult to find a way out. Using your breath as a tool to explore your deep emotions is incredibly valuable.

Always pay attention to your breath.

"Only you can be honest with yourself. Get down and collect your spirit. Push it down, and force it down with the air that you inhaled. "When it reaches your heart, you'll be amazed at the joy it brings you: you won't regret anything anymore," wrote a wise monk living in the thousand-and-three hundred.

Keep your hands on the chest. To isolate yourself, close your eyes.

Feel the heat coming from your body. Listen to your breath as it moves in and out. You can do this anywhere you want, at any moment, and slowly, you'll start to tune into your inner peace, in a peaceful, calm, inner balance.

Use your imagination to imagine your worst fears.

What color is your anxiety, and what do you think it looks like? What is the form of fear that you feel? Most recent research on the brain shows that people think in images. It can even be a benefit to choose language over imagination. Words go through us, and we flee, but images stay in our minds. Instead of running away, you become more aware of your fears.

Find a place of safety and comfort that allows you to be free. Slowly breathe and let your feelings deep down guide you. Important truths are revealed when we can observe ourselves.

Let's start with another exercise. While you breath, imagine a scene in the sky. What color is it? Depending on your mood and days, it may appear in different shades. All you have to do is observe the passing cloud moving away.

Relax and allow yourself to be free. Inhale while you imagine. Keep imagining, and let go all thoughts and worries. Your emotions are released as you merge with the sky and air, which is always there, regardless of how difficult it may seem.

Inhale slowly and exhale slowly.

Feel the light of colors envelope you. The air fills your nostrils and your lungs.

Be free.

Breathe.

Breathe.

Let the clouds do away with all your worries.

Breathe.

Everything is fine and everything is great.

Concentrate on your breathing.

Keep your eyes closed and let the air flow.

It is free.

You can even sleep.

Chapter 2: Breathing Is Life

Hello, how are your?

I would like you to be well. It is possible that after you listen to the first story in the book, you will already experience the first beneficial effects of your sleep through breath.

You don't have to worry if it isn't, because there are still lots of things you can do together. And, remember, Rome was not built in just one day! Wasn't it?

We are ready, then?

Are you happy in a comfortable place?

Do you want to do a great night's rest?

Okay, follow me. Don't forget to pay attention to what we're going to learn tonight.

It might be boring. But I want to keep my attention on breathing. You gave me confidence when I chose this book. Please don't underestimate the topics I will present to you.

Our inner balance can be found in our breathing.

The way we breathe can have an enormous impact on our body's physiological balance.

We'll be covering the basics of diaphragmatic and other breathing techniques, as well as how to do them.

Diaphragmatic breath is a type that strengthens the diaphragm. Also known as ventral breathing or abdominal breathing. This type of breathing is the base of almost all meditation and relaxation methods. It helps to lower stress levels, lower bloodpressure, and regulates important bodily processes.

It is because of modern lifestyles, such as stress, family, work and depression, that incorrect breathing occurs. This causes us to breathe mainly with our upper coasts and to keep an inspiratory bloc for the entire day.

So the diaphragm can remain at the bottom as an inspiratory bloc, while the so-called "additional muscles" must do a job that will actually serve the diaphragm.

To determine if your diaphragm functions properly, you can simply place one hand on the stomach and one on the chest. Inhale while you continue to breathe. Your belly will expand while your chest stays still. If you feel your belly expands, but your abdomen stays relatively still, that is an indication that your breathing is incorrect.

Fear not, you are part a large group that breathes primarily with the chest (nonphysiological).

Normal conditions call for inhalation to be from the Diaphragm (muscle–tendon foil separating chest cavity from abdominal cavity). Exhalation should be done passively except when the expiratory act must be forced. In that case, the transverse muscle in the abdomen would be called in.

Breathing through the chest can cause you to limit the movement and function of the diaphragm. There are many problems associated with chest breathing, including poor posture, breathing difficulties, circulation problems and lumbar pain.

Diaphragmatic breaths can also eliminate the harmful effects of chest air. Although diaphragmatic breathing is an integral part of meditation, it also has a direct influence on all other benefits. It can have incredible effects on both body and soul, even when not used in meditative practices. These are just a few of the benefits of this herb: It relaxes, reduces cortisol (the stresshormone) in your body, slows your heart beat, and is thus very beneficial for people with tachycardia. It lowers blood pressure, aids in coping with post-traumatic stress disorder symptoms, increases muscle stability and resistance to intense exercise. This makes it ideal for athletes and reduces the risk of injury.

It's possible to save energy by slowing your breathing.

Although there are many benefits, it is impossible to list them all.

Let's look at some very basic exercises to help diaphragmatic respiration.

Do not force yourself to breathe. You may feel dizzy or hyperventilated.

It takes just a few seconds a day to improve your body's well-being.

For those with anxiety and/or tenseness, it is best to get help from a qualified personal coach who will teach you correct breathing techniques in person.

However, it is strongly advised, especially for the first few attempts, and for people who are particularly anxious and withdrawing or insecure, pregnant women, or people with serious illness, to seek out a qualified personal coach who will help you in person.

You should also be calm and not force these movements through the use of your abdominal muscles. The process should be smooth and natural, without any tension.

Let's move on.

Like every other muscle, the diaphragm should be trained to maximize its potential.

You can loosen, stretch, or strengthen your diaphragm to dramatically alter the way your breathes.

Assume a supine position on the floor. To provide comfort, you may use a yoga mat, blanket, or a pillow.

Your legs should be bent and your feet should be positioned so that the width of your feet is equal to the width your shoulders. The plants should rest on the ground.

Now, relax your entire body and place one hand on each side of your stomach. The other is on your chest.

If that helps, you might also want to close your eyes.

Breathe through your nose. Try to only raise your hand from your belly each time you inhale.

Keep your eyes open and focus on your body.

Repeat for ten breaths.

Let's look at some exercises to strengthen our diaphragm.

These exercises are possible at any time during the day.

If you are unable to lay on your back, you can use a blanket, carpet, or support mat to help you.

Place both hands around base of rib cage. Thumbs should rest on sides of chest. Other fingers should extend along chest.

You may find that your fingers touch one another if you have a very small rib cage, or exceptionally large hands.

Your thumbs should be against the ribs to provide resistance.

Try to stretch your ribs so they press against you thumbs.

To begin, you should keep your eyes open to see your diaphragm expanding.

Take a deep inhale and gently pull your hands apart. Then exhale.

Continue to hold this position for 10 breaths.

Once the cycle has ended, you can stretch your arms out along your hips and then breathe ten additional times.

Continue the exercise for 2 more times.

Make sure to create a non-mechanical and harmonious movement.

You don't have to complete all of these exercises at once. Instead, you can choose to perform the first exercise as a bonus if you feel it is beneficial.

This is called "breathing with sand" Yes, you'll need a bag filled with sand and similar materials like beans or seeds to do this exercise.

You can lie on your back in a supine or prone position.

Slowly, place the bag under your breastplates. The bag should cover the entire area between the middle of your ribs and the abdomen, just below the navel.

You can direct your breathing to the bag by paying attention to where it is. Inhale and exhale as the bag gets higher and lower.

Don't lift your body by using muscles. Instead, breathe in slowly to increase your body until it reaches the point of lifting the bag.

Continue lifting the sack by your breath for ten seconds, then stop and rest until you feel the desire to do so again.

Repeat the process for two more times when you are comfortable.

Breathing stimulates our bodies to work more efficiently, and this is why it has such profound effects on our overall well being. The diaphragm organ plays a crucial role in breathing. It can stimulate, stimulate, and flood all surrounding organs and tissue with blood and oxygen when it is unaffected by any restrictions or alterations.

Diaphragmatic breathing, which is basically a way to improve your life, and meditation that starts from basic functions like breathing, are the best ways to meditate.

Remember, breathing is vital.

When you begin to pay attention and notice your reactions, your walking, and the way that you breathe, then you will be in a state called meditation. Meditation begins with a "far away" observation of yourself. When you pay more attention to your breathing, the real turning point is meditation. The moment you are conscious enough to start becoming more aware of yourself, then you can continue on a progressive path.

First, pay attention to your posture while you are walking. Normal walking requires you to turn your forearms towards the side and your shoulders forward.

This allows you to keep your chest open, and also prevents the formation of forward-curved shoulders.

It takes only a few moments to pay attention to oneself. For example, if you notice how your arms are positioned while you walk, this is the beginning of self-observation.

It is possible for incredible things to happen if you pay the same attention to your breath.

Breathing is such a powerful tool for mind control that mystics and spiritual seekers around the world have used it for thousands upon thousands of years as a way of calming the mind and allowing them to "beyond."

Attention to breathing can anchor you in the present moment even before your mind goes beyond it.

This allows you to be calmer and more effective in your everyday life. Your emotional and psychic life will be easier if you control your breathing.

The power is yours. Or, perhaps your conscious attention.

Your mind can be controlled by your breathing. This will reduce anxiety and stress. In this way, you can control your body and it will relax. It will then become calm, but also more energetic.

Your breathing pattern is what you choose.

Choose the abdominal/diaphragmatic pattern that gives you the calming effect you need to regain a clear thought and well-being of mind.

Your breathing pattern is what you choose.

Choose the abdominal/diaphragmatic pattern that gives you the calming effect you need to regain a clear thought and well-being of mind.

Do not eat anything but a full stomach. Your diaphragm will push against your stomach. This would stop you from relaxing. Breathing exercises should not be done with meals.

For those who attend a singing course or for those who are professional singers, the awareness in the use of the diaphragm is fundamental because the breathing that is considered functional for the sung voice is the cost-diaphragmatic (or thoraco-diaphragmatic). It allows the singers the ability to use the maximum lung capacity, while avoiding the muscle contractions that higher-breathing, such as upper costal and clavicular, can easily cause to the throat.

Proper breathing is key to any vocal improvement. With this, you'll be able have more energy, focus, calmness, and more power. Your vocal timbre will also increase. Just half of being a good singer is breathing. Many people believe that they sing by breathing with the diaphragm. In reality, however, one can breathe with the diaphragm throughout their day, including while walking, sleeping, and eating.

Everybody knows how tiny children can speak for themselves. Even though they started breathing only a few short months ago, How could they be so loud and shrieking for so many months without having any problems with their vocal cords?! Why can't their voices stop falling out? It all boils down to the way they breath. They only use one part of their diaphragm. They do not strain any muscle, as they are not yet strong enough to do so. All of us used the diaphragm to begin our lives. But, due to modern living conditions, it became less useful. It's not about learning to breath in an unnatural manner, but rather returning to breathing the way mother Nature has given us.

Good.

Now that we have discussed how to breathe with your diaphragm, let me show you another way to breathe so that you can choose the type that suits you best.

But, it is important to remember that the practice of one cannot exclude others.

Square breathing, also called square breathing, is an example of controlled breathing that can be used in yoga and other meditative activities. Let us now examine the techniques and benefits of square yoga breathing.

The options for execution are limitless and anyone can choose the method that suits them best. However, it is important to follow the timetable of four phases with equal duration. It is important to practice this technique at least five to ten times a day in order not only to improve your physical health but also your spiritual well-being.

What are the health benefits of square breathing

There are many benefits to the whole body. It can help you relax, release tension, increase oxygenation and promote inner harmony.

You can experience greater well-being, freedom and a renewed feeling of "freshness". You will feel like the sun is shining again on your skin.

Breathing in conscious and using a good technique will help you cope with any stress, difficulty, anxiety or fear. It will regulate the heartbeat, blood pressure, and calm the nervous systems.

Square breathing should be practiced in a comfortable posture, just like any other breathing technique, meditation, or yoga. The best way to do this is to sit down straightened with your legs extended, your hands on the floor, and your head aligned along your spine. As you breathe, you can promote relaxation and tension release by simply sitting down.

Square breathing should be easy and not cause fatigue. You might feel a little awkward at first if you have difficulty with breathing or are stressed. It is important to try to feel as natural or as easy as possible.

There are people who feel good about counting breaths, others who walk while doing it and can synchronize time according their steps. And there are those who do it with heartbeats. It is a common and well-known exercise to color the sides of a square. You can start from the vertical side and work your way down, each time you do the phases. Another option is to imagine a shape cyclically swelling and shrinking.

I encourage all of you to find your favourite method.

Let us now get into the details of the four steps needed to attain all the positive effects from square breathing.

The first phase involves inhalation. We count up to four. Depending on your level of preparation and mood, you can increase or decrease this time. The fourth second must bring the lungs to full capacity.

The second stage is the retention or encapsulation of air in our lungs. It is important that our lungs remain fully expanded with all the air we have taken in. This phase takes four seconds to complete, or as long as you prefer.

The third phase involves exhalation. It can be practiced by counting up from four or other times. The most important thing to remember is that you must reach the end with your lungs empty.

The fourth phase, or empty lung retention, is the final. After holding your breath for four seconds we resume phase one. This takes five to ten minute, but you don't have to force yourself or change your physical attributes. I highly recommend it.

It is simple, isn't?

You should feel confident that you can carry on this practice for as long as you like, and without feeling tired.

But, if you feel that your breathing is not in sync with your rhythm, you can end the practice and stop trying to balance it.

All the breathing exercises you have seen thus far will help to calm anxiety attacks.

You have many options for combinations with this breathing.

For example, you could draw squares clockwise once and counterclockwise once.

Or, you could imagine drawing the square twice in one color or once in each side in another color... Use your imagination to create your own squares.

You can also associate breathing with your heartbeat if that is what you desire, even if it is something you are already able to hear.

For a cue, you can inhale, pour right, then color the square pink. Hold your breath and exhale color purple.

If you feel like something is wrong, don't worry! You can just take a few minutes to breathe.

Breathing is a way to live better and to better manage our lives.

You can find inner balance to solve many of our problems. Balance is key to your ability to control life and problems. Because our breathing affects our behavior and actions, being in control of your breath can help you master the situations you're currently facing.

A few breathing exercises prior to bed will help to relax, oxygenate and induce sleep.

Focusing on the breath, as it has now been clearly stated, is one the best ways for you to forget about your worries, combat insomnia, and get some rest.

All the tension built up over the day becomes a knotty skein in the night, which causes insomnia. It is the inability of getting a deep and restorative sleep.

While it is common to suspect that this problem could also be due other chronic pain factors such as age or unhealthy lifestyle habits or other health issues, the majority of these problems are caused by stress or anxiety.

However, you can change your habits and practice the simple breathing techniques that I studied with you just before going to sleep to achieve the calmness and inner harmony that your brain requires to rest.

You can see the benefits day after day, no matter what your cause of insomnia.

I'll give you a quick summary.

Deep breathing and the use of numbers are without doubt among the best breathing techniques. They allow you to focus your attention only on breathing.

This will allow you to forget all of your worries, and make it easier to manage stress. Follow these steps:

You should lie on your back, straightening your spine.

Be comfortable and wear clothes that aren't too loose.

Deeply breathe in and count your breathing.

Take a deep breath and hold it.

Do this at most eight times.

Repeat the eight-minute cycle for five more minutes.

Diaphragmatic breathing, also known as abdominal breathing, is the traditional way to relax both mind and body.

It is useful not only to treat insomnia but also to reduce stress and improve attention, digestion, energy, and metabolism.

You can do it the following:

Sit on your back.

Place one hand on the abdomen and the second on the chest.

Breathe deeply through your nose. You will notice a swelling in the abdomen, diaphragm lowering and filling the abdomen as a result of the pressure.

Take a few moments to hold your breath, then exhale.

You can repeat this eight times. Rest for five to ten more minutes, and then you can start again.

Here we get to square breathing. This breathing technique seems almost amusing and is very easy. It is extremely beneficial and you will experience inner calmness and peace within ten nights.

This exercise will enable your brain to relax, and help you sleep better.

These are the steps.

First, find a comfortable position.

Take four deep breaths and visualize yourself drawing a side.

For four seconds, hold your breath while coloring on another side.

For four seconds, inhale and continue to add the third side.

Keep your breath on the square for four seconds, then close it.

Restart the cycle.

It is possible to create squares, even if you are not awake.

I want you to know that I am leaving you with a few last words.

All of the breathing techniques and exercises that we have used together are valid and useful. Although it might seem normal at first to be skeptical, this is normal. Even someone may have raised their eyebrows to express doubt and grimaced with their mouth as though to say "what nonsense!" It might even be worse: "It will never work with you!" I have no fault. I don't blame anyone. Human nature can be more than just normal. It is not uncommon to be distrustful of others and find it difficult to accept the solutions offered by them. However, I am certain that if you bought this book, it was because you felt that you could trust it. Most importantly, you understand that you require a method to solve problems.

You can start right now. Now prepare your mind in a way that will allow you to truly commit to this approach. Inspire your body, soul and spirit to get back the awareness we lost due the stress and chaos caused by our actions.

Be patient. Patient. Give yourself permission to be patient.

Do not believe that you can make a complete turnaround in a matter minutes. You need to put in the effort, persevere, and have a lot of willpower.

Do not lose heart.

Do not lose sight of your true self.

Don't stop believing in your abilities. Never.

You have extraordinary potential.

I'm not saying this to console, but because it is the truth. If you sense that you are in danger of falling, stop. Look for other ways to solve the problem, such as the one you purchased with this book. You may also consult experts if the tunnel is dark. Do me a big favor by giving it a shot. Do it for you. You deserve it. You are worthy of feeling good.

Would you like a start?

All right.

Close your eyes and breathe.

You can also begin to inhale deeply tonight and then practice the various techniques from tomorrow.

Feel at home.

You can place your hand on your belly to start listening.

You can take care yourself better than anyone.

Relax, let yourself go.

Let go of all thoughts and fall asleep.

Breathe.

Breathe deeply and let all the toxins go.

Be free from all the negative thoughts that cloud your emotions or your mind.

Don't be afraid to take control of your life.

You deserve order.

Get rid of toxins and clean your soul.

Let's get started!

Your nostrils will open as though they were the windows in the room.

Let go all the heavy air inside, and let it all out.

Breathe.

It is time to change the way you see the world.

Breathe in and let go to a new dimension.

Let everything get reorganized, cleaned, and brightened.

Breathe.

Breathe.

Chapter 3: Let Us Meditate On Meditation

This is our chance to share a moment of quiet and peace.

As I frequently recommend, you should be comfortable and create a relaxed and comfortable atmosphere around yourself.

Next, make sure to be comfortable. For example, you can wear a wide and soft pajama, loosen your hair, or take off your trouser belt if your are a guy.

Have you ever tried sleeping in socks before?

Okay, I get it. It isn't the highest level of eroticism. That's all right. However, thermoregulation is a mechanism that regulates body temperature. Feeling cold in your lower extremities does not help you sleep. Warm socks help the body maintain a temperature that is conducive to falling asleep fast. There are many nice socks out there today. It is worth looking for one with a funny design or the symbol of a super hero. Try it, you will be amazed.

Many people will make complex meditation speeches or assume that others, such as you dear reader may know what they are talking. I am a firm believer in involving others so that we can align on the same level.

What is meditation? What is meditation?

What does meditation actually mean? This is the question that you ask me. The simple answer is yes.

Meditation refers to something fundamental and simple, that is not connected to any culture.

So what is (and not!) meditation? meditation?

This definition is found under the heading "Meditate" in the vocabulary.

"To stop for a prolonged time and to concentrate with intense spiritual concentration the attention on an object or thought. To think deeply about a problem, argument in order understand its essence, investigate its nature, draw conclusions, etc. ".

For the uninitiated, these few lines might seem to convey an extremely complex concept. In fact, the practical side meditation is a mystery to those who have never experienced it. But they are a good starting point to understand the depth and reasons why it's worth trying to learn. Meditating can be described as a way to transcend, evolve, transform, avoid emotional stagnation, and prevent thoughts from becoming stuck. We must remain present and focused on the present moment.

Meditation is to simply be present and not dwell on worries, fears, or other unnecessary thoughts. Meditating is a way to enjoy the present moment. It also involves disciplining your mind to release it from its "autopilot". To contemplate the world around you and feel all the sensations, meditation allows you to meditate.

Many people have a wrong idea about meditation. For this reason, I want to clarify the meaning of meditation before anyone starts.

Meditation is not considered a religious practice. Despite being used in many religious rituals over thousands of years, it is still a practice that is closely tied to prayer. There is only one thing that meditation has in common: the discovery of one's inner spirituality.

Meditation is not designed to provide superpowers or mystical visions. Even though the stories of masters who were able to attain enlightenment (including the Buddha), are amazing, this can only happen with practice and is in no way guaranteed. Do not expect to be hypnotized by meditation or to be in a position to levitate in space. This would only make it more difficult to meditate and lead to frustration.

Meditation isn't something to do on a daily basis. To see the first results, it is important to meditate each day for at least a few minutes. Your patience and constancy are essential to success. I promise you that the rewards will be well worth it.

Meditation is, I repeat: being in an attention state. It's not about what you are doing but how you do.

Be silent, don't repeat mantras and don't mention God's name. Just be aware of your thoughts. Do not disrupt it, don't obstruct or suppress it.

Relax and just be present in the moment. You are here and now.

Clear vision.

Being connected with everyone.

Being aware, being present.

Meditation is peace, silence, listening and stability.

It doesn't mean to adhere to a method, but to connect to your natural state of being.

You can let go of your grip and relax into a state where you are calm. Is it something you would like to do?

These are our assumptions. We'll now show you how to meditate.

To start, stop everything.

"Stop" cannot be reconciled with our everyday lives. To meditate, you must stop.

It is important to find the best moments in your life that you can stop the inputs to your brain from every direction.

Are you going to walk to work? Or do you take the train along the regular route? This is a great opportunity to use it. You can turn off your phone, walk, and not think about anything. Then, after a few days, you'll start to notice that things have nothing to do. These are also the main principles behind walking meditation. This technique can be used for any activity, even housework.

You should focus on your spirituality.

Everybody has a spirit. But, our spirits are often muted by the daily evil that overwhelms and oppresses.

Learn to give meaning to words. Analyse what you hear, how you pronounce, read, or think about a word. Find its true meaning and use it in the right way. Learn to give words their real value. You may notice that I frequently greet you and ask your questions. Perhaps I begin the chapter by greeting you and asking how are you. Consider how you would answer my questions. There is no need to be worried about being clear or about making a good impression. You will only know the answer. Words matter, but if you pay close attention to them, you will find that there are many other things.

Your mind should not be focused on an object.

We have many possessions and always want more. This is part and parcel of our nature. But, how often do we stop and take stock of what we own? Or simply the fact that these items are our property, sat in a corner awaiting to be dusted or pulled from the bottom of a drawer.

Find an object that is near you. It can be an item in your home or your personal.

After you return home, take some time to let your mind wander as you look at the object.

The essence of everything is important.

It is important to capture the essence.

Do you still remember the object you spent a few days looking at? Now imagine where it came from, how it was made, the materials used and who it may have been handled by.

One example is a painting. Think about who it was painted, what the painter or artist felt while painting it, which colors he used for a starting point, and how he then proceeded to outline the landscape, various subjects, the light, shadows, and shadows. If it's wooden, you can also linger over the frame to see who carved it. Also, consider how the wood looked before it was polished and treated.

If you notice any marks on the object, remember where they came from. It could be a corner chipped in a move, a hole or trivial scratch.

Imagine being able to do all of these things with an object. Now imagine the moment when you will be able to attain the essence of people.

Investigate the natural order of things.

This modern era has given us much to learn about food. Although we are familiar with how to read labels, understand where food comes from, what the calories are, how do we savor it? Do we know the origins of the food?

Take some fruit and hold it in one hand. Now, imagine the tree, its earth, the sun that ripened them, and the care they required to complete the cycle. Enjoy it, and take the time to savor each bite.

When you stop and think about what we've done, it seems like a small amount. It didn't take you too long and it didn't make your life difficult. You started to see the difference. But, it was not obvious. With these consistent exercises, you became more aware of how to meditate.

Always consider the consequences.

Once awareness has been achieved, it is natural to start thinking about the consequences.

Every action, every word and every gesture has its consequences. Positive or negative consequences can have a multiplier effect that will lead to more complicated mechanisms.

It is hard to understand this advice and especially to follow it. But, anyone who wants to meditate knows that it is a difficult task to explore within ourselves.

You can think about the possible consequences of your reaction to a position or your gesture.

You don't have to do this, but it helps to think about the possible consequences. Sometimes, it helps to empathize. Place yourself in someone else's shoes, and imagine how you would react if you were there.

Harmony is your goal

We all know how annoying it is to hear a knife scratching on plates or hearing the whistles. These disharmonious sounds are disharmonious. The traffic noise, disharmonious people shouting into megaphones, disharmonious yelling, and I could go on.

Harmony is like water in the desert to meditate.

This is why we need to learn how to do it.

Find your space, where you feel comfortable. It could be in your own home or in a private space. Or, if you are a lover of walking, you could choose to walk in a forest or river. Enjoy a cup or a drink that you like, surround yourself by elements that will promote wellbeing, and take at least ten moments each day to let go of all the negative things that have happened.

It's a must-do treatment.

You deserve some personal time.

These tricks will make meditation easy for you once you master them.

Let's practice some more.

Let's first understand what the correct position is.

Meditating requires us to feel relaxed and upright while we are sitting. For energy to flow more easily and avoid drowsiness when meditation, it is essential to have a straight back.

To do this, tilt your pelvis forward and place the cushion on your back. You don't have to sit cross-legged the first time. However, it is a smart idea to do so to achieve the Vairocana Meditation position. This is the fundamental posture recommended for beginners and helps to maintain mental stability.

If you are unable to take this position, but you feel comfortable, sit in the closest place to you.

Perhaps it's better to clarify Vairocana's principles.

The lotus position is where the legs cross in a lotus position. This helps to reduce thoughts and improve circulation.

People who have used chairs and armchairs for years may feel intimidated when they see the idea of sitting down on the ground. But unlike the Orientals we didn't learn this from an early age. Our hips have evolved to accommodate the chairs. A meditation cushion that supports you is recommended before you try the lotus posture.

Pillows can be used on your couch or bed. But, you need to make sure it fits your body correctly and doesn't cause any pain.

It is important for you to remember that pain should not be felt when you take on this position. The knees, which are an extremely delicate part of the body, should not be overstrained.

It can be tiring for beginners or people who don't have the flexibility to move in the lower limbs. For these reasons, we recommend that you take it step-by-step. Begin with a warm-up and work on the easier variants. Next, practice the lotus position.

The lotus position requires extra attention for your knees and ankle joints. Prepare them by gently massaging them for a few minutes.

Place your right palm facing up in the left-hand, and place the tips of your thumbs gently on top.

The hands are approximately four fingers below each navel.

The right hand symbolises method and the left the wisdom. They are both connected in the course the meditative process.

Your back should be straight and not tense. This helps keep your thoughts clear and allows energy to flow more freely.

The lips are fully open and the mouth is relaxed. However, the tongue touches only the back of the upper arch of the dental crown.

This expedient reduces excessive salivation while also preventing dryness.

To prevent any mental arousal the head is slightly forward. The chin is slightly attached to your neck so that the eyes face downwards.

The eyes are half-open and you can see down to the nose.

Your eyes should be open so you don't become distracted. But, if your eyes are completely closed, you could easily drift off to sleep.

To improve air circulation, the shoulders are relaxed and level.

Vairocana's posture also features the preliminary breathing. This helps to place the mind in the right frame and "teach" the body how it can meditate. The moment we start meditation, our brain is filled with unhelpful thoughts. It's difficult to transform such a state into a peaceful, serene state. A disturbed mind is likened to a piece of black cloth. It cannot be dyed any other color unless it has been stripped of its base black.

It is crucial to eliminate all negative thoughts and distractions from our mind before we begin the meditative journey. You will temporarily be able achieve this through controlled breathing, as we have discussed.

After you have found a comfortable place on your meditation cushion and are able to focus, notice what thoughts and distractions are running through your mind.

Now, focus your attention on your breathing and allow its rhythm to remain normal.

As you exhale imagine removing all thoughts and distractions from your mind by inhaling black smoke, which disappears into the distance.

Think instead of taking in all that is good and inspiring about creation.

Keep this vision active twenty one times every inhale/exhale. This will keep your mind calm and alert until you are able to focus on the present.

Adopting this expedient will make it temporarily impossible for negative thoughts or distractions to return.

At this point, your mind will feel like a blank white canvas that you can color using the many colors the meditative practice will offer to your spirit.

You may now be curious about the benefits of meditation in daily life, even though you have already learned the basics. This is a valid question. It's normal to desire to see the benefits of meditation, even in the short term. We also want to "touch them" with the daily challenges we face. Your journey will begin with better control over your thoughts and emotions. You will also notice a peaceful mind and less worry. Interfacing with your normal commitments will show you this. You'll find that emotions like anger, nervousness or mental confusion appear much less frequently, until they vanish almost completely.

If you practice meditation regularly and improve your technique, these benefits can be transferred to many other areas of your lives, such as your relationships with others and your own spiritual and physical health. You can also benefit from specific sessions to help you in many other ways. While meditation will not cure serious health problems, it isn't and won't be an effective treatment. It serves as a strong support for those suffering from psychosomatic issues that are caused primarily through our emotions.

Science and millions of people have proven the many benefits meditation can bring to our lives. Yet, despite the numerous benefits that daily meditation can bring, many people still believe that meditation isn't right for them.

Let's face it: meditation is something that everyone can do. To meditate, our awareness and our mind are the only things needed.

Even though this is true, our mental schemas often work against us and make us feel inept and inadequate. Perhaps you are just starting and worried about making rookie mistakes or not getting it right. Long-term, you may be wondering why your meditation progress is slowing down and want to give up.

Perhaps you meditate just occasionally or daily, but it isn't working as well as you expected. You may even feel that your meditation isn't working as well as you thought and doubt its effectiveness.

You are not alone.

Let's see what the most common and worst mistakes are, and how we can meditate to avoid them.

Lack of consistent practice.

This is probably the most common reason that your practice isn't moving forward.

To make a lasting difference in your life, meditation should be practiced each day. It is obvious that every time you meditate you are able to experience some benefit. Consistent practice is the key to mental and emotionally transformation.

You should aim for constancy when you're learning how to meditate. Not the amount of time you spend sitting down or how straight your legs are. Spending ten minutes per day is better that spending half an hour every other week.

Your mind is constantly working, so it's important to keep your mental patterns in check, even seven days a week. That's why it is important that you improve your ability meditate every day. I will now focus my attention on habit.

It is easiest to establish this habit by starting to meditate before you eat breakfast in the morning. Begin by meditating for two minutes each day, if needed. But, be determined not to skip a day no matter what.

Do you have a hectic day? Do you have a busy day?

Do you have questions about your posture or whether you are doing it correctly?

Do not overthink it, just do it anyway. Later you will be able to verify if it was done correctly.

Take the view that no external or internal circumstance can hinder your meditation efforts.

Too much is expected too quickly.

It was probably the expectation of numerous benefits that prompted you to choose this book and begin meditating. Once you have established the habit of meditation, it's time to stop worrying about the benefits and start to meditate simply for the enjoyment of it. Every day you should shower, eat, then sleep.

How can you overcome this mental predisposition

You can relax and have fun when you meditate. Relax and enjoy the feeling you have after you get in position. You'll feel calmer. While meditation may not always feel idyllic, if you have been practicing it for a while, you will find that you experience a surprisingly positive feeling after only one session.

The deeper benefits of meditation can only be realized after years or months of consistent practice. You must let go of your expectations to keep practicing meditation. Every now and again. Every day, we run in order to get to work on-time, catch the train, cross the street, or avoid the red traffic light. There is no traffic signal here. The road is straight. All you have to do is enjoy the ride.

Do not practice before you are ready.

You can sit down at any time and meditate as you would anywhere else in the world. However, your session can be much more productive if your body is relaxed and your mind calmed.

You don't need to be complicated. All you need is to stretch for three seconds, take three deep breathings, and say your intention: "Okay, now let me concentrate for ten minute." This can be done before you have to get up in the morning, before you start your breakfast, or even before you wake the family.

Jumps from technique in technique

It's a good idea to try new techniques in your first months. Later, you can either study deeper or practice a guided meditation every day. It is better to stick to the technique you are most comfortable with after the first few months.

Can you imagine an apprentice cook cooking thousands of different dishes all at the same time? It would be a mess at the stove. A dish that burns, forgets an ingredient, or causes other issues would not taste great. You should learn each skill slowly so that you become comfortable.

Each person is unique, so there is no one meditation method that is more effective than the others. It is important that you try several techniques before you choose the best. For a few weeks you can try the technique to get an initial feeling of the effects. At the end, it is vital to identify the best technique and keep it. There is no perfect technique. You will find the one that works for you.

Concentrating on something, be it your breathing, or simply the act of unplugging your mind, can make that element more "charged" with energy and attention. Your mind will become more familiar with the element, which makes it easier to focus on it in future sessions.

You doubt whether you're doing it right.

Because you care deeply about your practice, and you want it to succeed, you may be prone to over-analyze. Unfortunately, this is a bad thing. Too often, we are our worst critics.

The self-criticism you make about your practice has two problems.

First, it keeps your mind busy while you practice by analysing your mental states. It is not letting it get lost in the meditation process.

Self-criticism is a common way to lose motivation. If you find yourself concluding that you aren't doing it well or cannot understand it, then you may give up.

You must practice, regardless of how difficult it may seem. Practice, practice and practice some more. The only way to be clear about meditation is through time. Consciously, it becomes more than a process that you need.

Keep your curiosity alive. Keep learning. Keep going regardless of your uncertainties with strength and courage.

You should be able to recognize distractions as soon as they occur. In your first few weeks, you may find your mind drifting for up to two or five minutes before realizing you are distracted. Gradually, you will become more aware of your surroundings and reduce the gap. This is awareness.

Secondary goal: To keep your attention on your object in meditation, moment to moment. Although you might only be able keep your attention on the object of meditation for three seconds at first it will get easier over time. But patience, willpower and practice will help you increase your focus. This is concentration.

Do these two things the best you can, then high-five! This is meditating.

Inexperienced practitioners often make another mistake. They don't give enough attention to the practice and do not intend to.

Sloppy exercise is a sign that you're not getting the most out of it. You cannot avoid eating a bad dessert if you make a mistake in a recipe. Meditation is the exact same. Meditation requires intensity, concentration, and determination.

Meditation is a practice that can be done with a greater commitment and intention. Your mind will feel calmer, more engaged, and therefore, better rewarded.

Don't treat meditation as just another task on your to do list. With reverence, sit as if your meditation is the most important activity of the day.

Do not rush to finish your task. Instead, breathe deeply, then wait a while before you slowly emerge from the meditation. This allows you to keep the experience with your throughout the day.

It is okay to get distracted. It is normal. It may take several months, or even years, before most people can experience meditation without any distractions. Never be too hard on yourself, just take a note of the distractions and let it go. Self-criticism will only take you one step farther from meditation. Be happy that you've noticed your distractions, as though it were a victory, and then just return to your object of mediation. You can treat yourself with kindness.

We will also discuss kindness in a more targeted manner in the pages that follow.

We tried to find inner balance by reading this book or using other methods, but we realized our mind is too busy all the time.

Meditation is necessary among other reasons. Your mind is too agitated and out of your control. Your mind wanders off course and is often affected by the expectations of society, family and institutions. If you keep repeating negative conditioning, you can often become less productive or less satisfied.

Your meditation's quality can have an impact on how your mind behaves during the day. The way you think about meditation can also affect your ability to meditate. No matter how deep or well-executed your meditations may be, some people will struggle to get rid of sixteen hours of worry and restlessness after twenty minutes.

Let me show you an example. Imagine if thirty minutes of cleaning were ineffective if you didn't throw garbage around the house, and maintained a constant state order. Meditation is similar. Meditation can only help to partially remove destructive thoughts and addictive emotions.

Be observant of your mind and observe what is happening within you. This will help you to develop a healthy habit. It is impossible to do this better than you. Only you can have the best perspective of yourself. This will improve your meditation and make the process of meditation easier. It is a positive, self-sustaining cycle.

Last, but not least: I have to point out the frequent exaggerated media consumption.

Media can create or increase anxiety. Movies, news, social media, articles, forums, games, TV, etc... This is a difficult challenge that meditation has never had to face in the past.

The brain is exposed to so much information that it is easy to see all the images and ideas when we meditate. This triggers distracting emotions as well as further reflection. Most of the media that we are exposed has been designed to cause us to feel restlessness, anger or fear.

You can transform your mental and/or emotional state by limiting the amount of media you consume. Take a moment to think about how you feel about what you see, hear, and read every day. I am not asking for you to erase your social media accounts or stop watching TV. Maybe you can try some "media fast" on weekends or just one day per week.

These habits can positively influence your meditation, as well as make you less stressed and more productive. You will be more present now without distractions and not feel obligated to take part in the virtual world.

Take one step at a time to address these "meditation error" issues if you are ever caught up in them. You can calmly work on the difficult ones, or those that have the most impact, by taking small steps.

Meditation is something that you must do for your entire life. As a child, how many times did you fall from your bike? How many times did your fall? How many times were you knocked down, hurt, or angry while your friends were out walking around the block? With the help of a guide (a parent or brother as this book can be), you were able to calmly do it. The bike went on the road. You got up and started pedaling. Even though you've been away from a bike for many months, you still have the ability to ride a bicycle.

What would it be like to be able meditate?

As we can see, it takes time to change the way the mind works.

Okay, I'm glad I helped you find the courage to start.

It's easy to start.

This is where you won't be judged, there will not be any expectations about your performance, and there will also not be any competition. It is something that you can do for your self, and only for yourself.

Meditation is a practice that can be done by anyone. Anyone can do this. Everyone can learn from their mistakes and make improvements.

The trip will be memorable if your confidence is high and you can trust yourself.

Chapter 4: How To Cultivate Inner Balance In A World Always In Hurry. Personal Growth, Respect, Awareness, Self-Esteem

I was required to visit the mall today to buy a birthday gift for a good friend. I don't often go to shopping malls or other crowded places. But this time, it was something I could not resist.

Even though it was a simple task of finding a store in a particular brand to buy the object my friend requested, I did manage to come across the order within the hour I spent on the activity.

A motorist was unhappy that I had moved my car closer to the entrance. He considered it elegant and appropriate, and dazzling and honking to show his appreciation.

In a guy who ran who knows how, pushed me violently onto the escalator, without even making an apology.

Finally, there was a saleswoman clearly bored or whipped her by his work who thought it was outrageous that I needed to get advice on color choice and then snorted loudly at the request for a giftbox.

Oh, poor me. I returned to the car with a heavy heart thinking that this could've been a fun outing if people weren't so negative. I could have wandered around the stores all day, considering I had spent some time for this commission. There were so many options.

Most likely, however I found that most of the people I encountered along my route were also affected by negativity. It's easy to fall into a vicious circle.

The bottom line is that everyone talks to you about balance and inner peace. Even the windows at a perfumery invited you to go inside to do a makeover session or to smell the new scents inspired by spring. But, the world seems inviting us to rush, to anger, and to arrogance.

We live in a reality that is full of hit and ran news, especially negative ones. These are baked minute to minute and cling tightly to us with all their cruelty.

The same holds true for others: Most of our friends don't tell us about the happy times they had, but only about the most recent trouble they went through.

Isn't it absurd?

So, how do we not cancel all of our inner work and get rid of the negative thoughts while still maintaining our serenity?

It took me years before I understood how to deal with negativity. Although we cannot all live in a treehouse on a peaceful island, or escape our responsibilities, we can reduce the stress and frustration we feel every day with some simple measures.

These tips cannot be considered a "magic recipe" or a universally effective method. However trusting in others and having some strength can work for us all in any situation.

Indifference, sincerity and honesty are my ingredients to inner peace.

Sometimes you must be indifferent, even at the expense of appearing cynical.

Even if it means you appear unfriendly or politically incorrect, your sincerity is essential.

If you don't want to appear outlandish or contrary to the dominant thought trend, it is okay to be honest.

This is my daily routine and my rule of life.

I've always believed that for the inner potential of each human being to shine, silence is necessary and courage must be used.

Below you will find some tips and tricks to "prevent" the negative influences that affect our inner well-being, as well as our overall balance.

Now imagine us sitting down at a dinner table, drinking, and you are listening to this advice as if it were your most trusted friend.

That's exactly what you want me to be right now.

Let's begin by being indifferent.

You should look into the causes of any inconveniences that you may experience in your life. You'll see that almost all cases have false expectations.

Did you notice that meditation is essentially a way to get rid of everything?

Understanding that the tragic events that occur are beyond your control is crucial. You need to let go of the situation to allow yourself to think clearly and be able to take action before they end. This is the source of your indifference. Not the kind that makes it difficult to be understanding and compassionate, but the constructive type that allows one to see the situation objectively with reason and clarity. You'll be able find the most suitable solutions to suit your personality and personality precisely this way.

It may seem like the easiest thing to do in the world to be sincere. But, if you really think about it, sincerity can only be appreciated when it touches you emotionally or privately.

You can only improve yourself if you are sincere, by knowing your limits and trying not to cross them, looking at the flaws of others and learning from them.

Do the same for others, especially those you care about. Don't be afraid of being honest, no matter what the outcome. Share with them your goals and challenges. Be respectful but not too prescriptive. Although this is hard, it will not be easy. People will be angry at you, and many will try to avoid you. But, these reactions can serve as a filter. You will eliminate negativity from your life that saps your energy. People who will not leave, but are curious about what you are saying, may ask you the reason. This will allow them to grow their awareness.

Honesty is a virtue, but honesty is a must, especially when it comes to your own principles, duties, and feelings. You don't have to "try not to get away" with the voice inside your ego. Instead you need to be honest with it.

Do I really try my best?

Are you trying as hard to be as good as you promised yourself?

What are my best options for my well being and me?

We all make mistakes. But, in order to see what we don't want and what our goals are, we must be honest about it all. It helps us to grow.

Do not listen to anyone who is constantly complaining about everything.

While being honest may not be popular, it is a way to look in the mirror and smile.

Honesty is embarrassing for all those who blink and don't side, who try hard to get in your way because they don't want to do it, or who are unwilling to take responsibility.

Being truthful means being honest with yourself and others.

Learn to gradually apply these three precepts to your life.

You'll notice how negativity slips away over time. You will see it with your own eyes. And you'll feel the impact of your serenity and transparency on the lives of others.

Your inner balance will help you to be a beacon in the storm.

Wait! Wait!

How can you recognize negative people?

Negativity or harmful people are not always reflected in obvious and unremarkable behaviors such as shoveling down a hallway, refusing to open the elevator doors to let you board, talking loudly on the cellphone in museums, etc. People can be much more deceitful than we think.

The real question here is not, "How do you recognize them?". Instead, ask yourself: "How can I manage them?"

It is obvious that evil exists in this universe, as well as the fact that good exists.

The difference between good and bad is that they are often done without effort. Good requires effort, heart, art, and effort.

The bad gets out of control, while the positive is rarely noticed.

To this end, gratuitous wickedness can be a problem that most of us have faced at least once. The negative vibrations we feel from angry or frustrated people every day stick with us like fried food. They make us more stressed and less productive. These people are often condescending and full of envy, anger, and hostility towards others.

You should not ask how to identify them. The real question should be: how do we manage them?

You won't find anyone who will challenge you or point out things you don't like about yourself to plot against you. People who have the guts to share their views with you and make constructive criticism are usually honest and loyal.

While there are exceptions, people do sometimes enjoy criticizing others in an attempt to make their mark. But it takes some cunning and it's not widespread.

Positive people, those who really believe it, are not dependent on malice or devious means to obtain what they desire.

Recognizing and separating bad behaviour from constructive criticism is a crucial step in neutralizing it.

You are most likely bringing out your deepest inner self by embarking on a meditation path. This will help you learn to recognize the signals from your instincts and to be more open to them. This extraordinary inner power is what you must use to quickly grasp an individual's behavior or attitude.

As per usual, I'll give you an illustration that will help to clarify the concept. Now imagine you're in a room with a stranger. How do you act?

Intuitively, your eyes will be drawn to the person. Next, you'll pay attention to his speech, accent, words, and pronunciation. But if you pay more close attention, something will happen that causes you to "perceive" if you like the person in front. It is a feeling you feel in the first moments. This instinctive feeling is temporary and you can be distracted from your brain, logic, reasoning, or stories. However, it is important to understand how to preserve this alert.

Your instinct, which is the most basic part of you, is often the one you don't recognize. But it always warns of the dangers. Sometimes, we do not listen to our instincts and do something we did not intend to. Most of the time however, we cancel what comes to us spontaneously due to our senses of duty or another solution.

Let's be clear. I don't want to make slogans like "the first impression matters" or contradict ancient sayings like "a beard is not a philosopher". Paying attention, paying attention and being attentive, listening to what is around you, not allowing things to happen by accident, are my words.

There is probably no magic formula for eliminating bad things or people.

There are many powerful weapons, and as we have seen in the cases discussed, they are all part of us. Knowing how to use them is all that is required. I'm referring to dialog. It is important to speak, explain your thoughts and feelings to others. Facing up to fearful conversations is a good idea. Bring out all the negative events that have happened to you, and explain why they made you feel so ashamed and hurt. Your positivity can help you fight the evil people.

You may not always be believed. You might not get satisfaction or benefits from your sincerity. But you will have reached a great goal: peace with yourself.

Instead of accumulating negativity in your mind, give it a channel of release. You will discover how much dialogue can be helpful for your mental equilibrium. And sometimes, you may even be able to reverse unfavorable circumstances through your emotional transparency.

Okay, okay. We are adults.

I know what your thinking. The bad guys continue to pursue their diabolic plans. But the right guys, or better yet, the right ones, will stay where they are.

I won't deny that it happens, but it is something that you are doing. It is to get rid of negative thoughts.

We would have a better world if it was easy, don't we think?

It's a mission that will completely change your life and your perspective.

If you don't feel like engaging in dialogue right away due to circumstances such as work, you will find two more ways to get your mind clear.

Be kind first. Harmful people will try to harm you with their weak points, aren't they? They will be happy to see you angry, sad, and misplaced. It will also double the bad things they do against your. Instead, you should respond with kindness and a smile even to the most vehement comments. You will confuse them.

While they may not initially understand the cause of your reaction, they will try to increase the dose. Do not succumb to temptation. Be strong and always ready to protect yourself. Use kind phrases that are appropriate for each situation. Or just smile and be spontaneous.

Let me tell you a quick example. It's a Monday morning and you see a colleague who is very negative. He says: "You know, that haircut age[s] you a lot." This time, instead of being disconcerted and offended, you can smile politely, saying "oh, thank you, and I'll talk with my hairdresser. But if you have any suggestions I would gladly take them." Boom! Boom! First, she or he will not expect you to show consideration. Then again, it may be that they are expecting to have some fun with haircuts. Can you just imagine how many giggles this will bring?

This doesn't mean you have to fight fire with fire. I recommend that you smile and don't take the blame for others. It is a mistake to become savage and mean to "revenge" others. Our mind is wired to seek peace and inner balance.

Let's try to look at this phenomenon with a wider lens.

Did you put up with bad people and situations for a long period of time because you were taught that you can't quit until you are insane or that resistance is necessary to build character?

If you can't answer the question with a "no", you are very lucky.

Sometimes, our emotional well being is subordinated to the needs that are more important. You don't have to worry about your own well-being; there are others who depend on you in some way.

What number of couples remain in a unhappy relationship because they don't want to be a nuisance to anyone else? Maybe you wait years to find your dream job, or you settle for a place that you don't like and are unhappy. You may keep in your drawer the business plan or the book you want to write and hope to find the time later.

The background sound is always the identical: "It's just that I feel so terrible right now!"

There are many situations where we prefer to stay put than fight or run away. We fear change. Paradoxally, we would rather stay in a position of stability, which doesn't make our happy or inspire us, than to have to get back into the game.

Even small frustrations can build up, resulting in small doses anxiety, fear, discomfort and anger that eventually lead to a lot of them. All negative emotions are not allowed to be suppressed and then buried by a seemingly corrective action. They are sometimes thrown out with great pain and severe consequences.

You can always do something to avoid becoming complacent and adapting at every cost. It's not rebellion or needing to change the world. Acceptance of change is what you need. It is possible to make new decisions, to act freely and to learn from your mistakes.

While it isn't an easy path, it can be done. It is important to make time for yourself. You should also be able to devote time to meditation. If you are able to cultivate self-esteem as well as respect and affection for yourself, then you will be able stop accepting every situation passively and increase your determination to make it better.

Don't worry.

You'll be great.

Chapter 5: Does Fasting Make You More Able To Meditate Well?

Wow! This is a hard subject to handle.

When fasting is associated with meditation, you must be extremely careful.

Fasting, attention is not to be confused w/ diet. It is certainly a tool we have at our fingertips to meditate better but also to feel more well. However, this is one of the most challenging challenges to tackle and must be done with great care.

But before I go on, let me clarify that this only applies to people who are healthy, stable, free of disease, and not pregnant.

In this regard, I like what I can say: It's one thing to meditate in the mountain cuckoo; another is to include a meditation path among our many commitments.

I remember the first tragicomic fast. It brought me so much enthusiasm and eagerness to do it again, even though I had no idea of the facts. I was going to run some errands in my car when I felt the sensation of fainting due to the dramatic drop in sugar levels and energy.

A strong mental motivation is essential to approach fasting. It may not necessarily have to be tied to meditation. Let me elaborate: If I must fast for twenty-four hour because I have a medical examination, I will always remember food and drink I cannot access. This will make it twenty-four exhausting and long hours. If I really want to, I can force myself to stop eating for twenty four hours. I need to wear a dress that highlights my waist. I will then think about the end result rather than the food. The state of your mind is what makes the difference. Okay?

We all know how vital food is to our daily lives. It's a great story.

Fasting is a way to give rest to overworked parts of the body that make up the machinery. It also allows us to be more alert and aware than all other sensations. It is enough to abstain for 24 hours from eating to reactivate the sleepy neurons. In order for our body's defense against stress, we need to take some precautions that will eventually protect our tissues.

A time when you are not eating can reduce and curb internal inflammation processes. It also improves your immune response and boosts the cells' ability remove toxins and waste substances. It is a true process of body purification, and should be carried out at regular intervals to improve our health.

Let me return to my personal experience. After the "tragicomic" first attempt, I talked to a friend of mine and he gave me some tips. Slowly, I reached the much-sighed three days fasting.

This is what happened to me: After the first day, I started feeling pain in some of my bodies. You should know that pain indicates a tired organ. This can indicate that you have deficiencies or weaknesses that are manifested in a lack of nutrition. Fasting is a great method to find your weaknesses, and then to rectify them.

Fasting causes your mind to be lighter and allows you enter deeper meditation phases.

You must be free from any disease or illness to be able fast. This is a rule that I would repeat again.

Also, I advise that you take this journey very slowly and consider your eating habits as well as your physical condition. Watch out for any special events, like a trip to a beach with your family or a wedding invite with reception. You can shift your fasting times to more favorable times. This may sound obvious, but it is important that you do not leave anything to chance.

For example, if your usual meals include breakfast, lunch, dinner and dessert, you could start your fast at lunch. This would eliminate dinner and allow you to continue fasting until dinner the next day. You can drink water during these hours and orange juice if you need it. You can also use that time to meditate, instead of eating at the table.

After fasting for eighteen hours the first week, increase your time by adding a few hours each week, depending on your needs. Skip breakfast in favor of breakfast the next morning, but continue drinking plenty throughout the day, even hot beverages like tea and herbal tea.

There are legitimate routes. I recommend, however, that you listen carefully to every signal coming from your body.

Fasting can have many benefits. One of the best ways to be in touch with yourself and test your self control is through meditation. When combined with fasting, it becomes an even stronger tool for self-awareness.

This will allow body, mind, spirit, and heart to be in perfect harmony.

Did you know that "mens' sana is corpore-sano" means "mens' sana in sano?"

It means a happy mind in a healthy person.

Chapter 6: Mantras, What They Are, How They Can Be Used, Why They Are Important

Hey, how's it going?

As we are all together now, I encourage you to take deep breaths, maybe drawing on the dictations from previous chapters. Then, relax and feel at ease.

Meditation and its various components are topics that you can benefit from learning. You are doing something to alleviate stress, anxiety, depression and melancholy, which affect millions of people each day. Simply because you are seeking relief, it is clear that you have found the right place. Take heart, be happy, and rejoice in this first step towards harmony within yourself.

The mantra is one among the most effective meditation aids. The practice of mantra meditation can be found in many contemplative traditions throughout the world. It has a rich history.

Here we will discuss together the different methods of meditation using mantras. We will also learn how to pick the best mantra for you.

Let's begin by defining mantra. Mantra is a Sanskrit phrase that comes from two roots. Mantra means "mind" (or "think") and "trai" which means, "protect," "free form," or "tool". Mantras, also known as tools of the mind, are tools that can help you free your mind.

They can be either a single word or a combination of words to help us meditate more effectively and bring spiritual benefits.

Some mantras have a literal interpretation and can be translated. But most of them, tradition says, derive their value mainly through the quality of sound. Some are shorter, one-syllable mantras while others are more complex and have many words.

Sometimes the mantra is recited. Other times it is heard. Sometimes the mantra must be repeated quickly and sometimes slowly. Sometimes, it can be just recited, but other times it has to be repeated in combination with concentration, breathing and chakras. Later, we'll see what the chakras actually are, visualizations or abstract concepts.

Many mantras, as well as related practices, are rooted within Hinduism, Yoga and Buddhism.

If you are suspicious, this might prompt you to wonder: "What is so special about repeating one word?" It is considered a powerful tool in meditation.

You are here to learn.

The basic idea is sound is vibration. Every cell in your body vibrates. Everything in the universe vibrates according to its own rhythm. Your thoughts and feelings are, in reality, the vibrations that your body and consciousness produce.

Sound patterns also have an effect on the water you drink, your hormone secretion, cognitive function, and your psychological well-being.

If you think about it this way, your mind (or rather your psyche) is a collection sound waves that each vibrate at its own frequency and speed. Yoga and mystics discovered that the mind and body could be transformed by listening to a specific sound vibration for long periods of time.

Each musician and director will confirm the extraordinary power of sounds, their ability and ability to affect moods, thoughts, emotions. Imagine how listening to a song can affect your mood and your ability to heal.

The idea is that mantras, as a key tool for the mind, can help create profound changes within your body and mind and lead to altered states. Mantra meditation can be described as a way to focus your consciousness on one sound and amplify it to produce an exponential effect. Mandatory meditation is a popular way to attain radical benefits. It's often simple and secure in the contemplative tradition.

Practice is more important than thinking.

Our attention can only focus on one thing at a particular moment. Even though we say we are multitasking, our minds are not focused on multiple mental actions at once. Instead, we only quickly switch from one object to the other. Multitasking is dispersive and ineffective.

This is the connection that meditation uses: When you pay attention to the mantra and aren't distracted by thoughts, memories, feelings, or other thoughts, it can be difficult to meditate. When you are able increase the amount of awareness between the end of each mantra repetition, and the beginning of the next one, you will be able to remain in a constant state of alertness for the duration of your meditation. It is not easy, but anyone can do it.

You could also achieve this through breathing or visualization. However, the main advantage of a mantra is its ability to replace our inner discourses, which helps to thin the clouds that cloud our conscious thinking, which is most people's predominant mode of conscious thought. Another benefit is that the mantra's rhythmic nature helps us to overcome the repetitive melodies playing in our heads. For example, an advertising jingle could be listened to endlessly on the radio, at the supermarket, in the car and even in the car.

Why repeat a mantra every day?

Trust me, the benefits to reciting a mantra is many. The benefits of reciting a mantra include deep relaxation, which is more than just normal relaxation, a substantial increase in happiness hormone production, and an increased self-awareness.

How to choose your mantras in meditation

What approach you take to meditation, secular or spiritual, will play a major role in choosing which mantras to use. It will also impact the outcome of the practice.

Some mantras can however be used with both the traditional and modern approaches. Sanskrit mantras such as om eso ham are an excellent example.

Reciting a mantra with a meaning you understand well is my first advice. It's easier to remember and vibrate with the mantra.

Let's look at five mantras to help you get started. These mantras are easy to access and can be very inspiring.

OM

It is undoubtedly the most commonly used mantra, invoking our divine aspect. It is something you have probably heard in many media channels, possibly even in the movies, and which, due to new-age philosophy, has become increasingly popular. It is possible to try this if you feel it appropriate. Just keep your back straight, close your eyes, and pay attention to your breathing. Next, we will mentally repeat the phrase for about ten more minutes. Reciting the mantra will help you to relax and restore your balance. To believe, try it!

The Rosary of the Russian Pilgrim and the Mantra Of The Russian Pilgrim.

These mantras are especially appropriate for Catholics. The rosary is particularly helpful for meditation because of its long duration. You can also fully immerse yourself in the words and vibrations.

The Russian Pilgrim's mantra instead is: "Lord Jesus, have mercy on me." This mantra reminds us of our mortal condition before God, and is not a cause for guilt.

Peace and Love

In order to move towards a lay dimension I'd like to propose this mantra: "Peace and Loving". It is a powerful mantra that invokes two key concepts to achieve personal and universal balance. You can also use these two words to breathe, inhaling and exhaling on each other. The result is to absorb peace as well as return love. You won't feel any better hearing these words.

I am him, So Ham oder So Hum

The So Ham mantra is a powerful sound that helps strengthen meditation. Indian masters have often called So hum (with a u in place of an a) "cosmic sound". There are two forms of So hum: one is female and the other male. So represents the "yin" nature. Hum the "yang" nature. While meditation, repeat the So ham mantra to help your mind stop wandering. The mantras serve as tools that help us achieve mental clarity, and offer great psychological benefits.

So ham, which can be translated as "I'm him", refers to an inextricable connection with God. You inhale by saying "So", which refers to the inner dimension. Inhaling, it's pronounced Ham. This sounds outward. The mantra is repeated by continuing to breath calmly and consciously.

When thoughts start to take over, the mind is drawn back towards the breath and repetition of the mantra. The So Ham mantra is repeated and breathed in, connecting us to the universal energies. This connection with the universal energy supports and sustains us. It is why the concept "unity" was born between the individual, the cosmos and themselves. The mantra can be repeated either mentally or in a voice. Repeating the mantra by voice will cause the vibrations to spread throughout your body, resonating in harmony with the energy within the internal organs. This meditation helps to calm the mind, and it creates an inner peace.

Let yourself be inspired now and use the mantra that is most meaningful to you. You can do it! Don't be afraid! A mistake will help to clarify what you want.

Don't worry, my hand is still on your shoulder. I will help you select the right mantra for you.

Lay approach

This view of meditation refers to it as a tool. An unbelievably useful exercise, developed and used in order for you to have better health, mental performance or relaxation. This does not necessarily mean you are a believer in meditation's spiritual aspects, whether they be God, enlightenment, or life after death. Perhaps you do believe it, but your meditation is not connected to the spiritual sphere.

I would recommend you choose a mantra that is in your native tongue. It could be a single phrase or one word that conveys a message.

Here are some guidelines to help you choose the right word.

First, you must understand what the word means. Pick a word/phrase that represents something that you would like to learn more about yourself or to which it is important to have a deeper connection. It could be love. Peace, freedom. Awareness. Courage. It may seem trivial to some. Why should it matter? You'll be perfectly content.

The sound must please you. Don't be affected by external factors. Try to use the word for yourself. Take a few moments to look at yourself from different angles. Does it feel right?

Do me a big favor: Avoid words with unclear meanings or potential negative connotations.

Try several mantras before choosing the right one. You should choose the best mantra to help you grow your effects over time.

Spiritual Approach

You can choose your mantra differently if your meditation has a purpose. The fact that every word contains its "energy", a result of the repeated use it has received from others, can be considered. A traditional mantra is one that spiritual researchers have used for many centuries, with excellent results.

It is absurd to translate the mantra into another language in this situation. It is preferable to use the original word as it was discovered or conceived in the language that it was written, such as Sanskrit. You must also ensure that the mantra is correctly pronounced and intonated.

The first step in deciding which cultural or spiritual tradition is most important to you is to determine your personal experience. Spend some time researching these traditions to discover the one that most closely relates to you.

You should keep your mantra secret in this way, even though it may seem strange to some people. Secrets are sacred, inviolable, necessary, and therefore, they are considered sacred. You will feel deeper effects if you treat your mantra like a secret.

We now have some practical guidelines to help you meditate with a mantra. These guidelines are also applicable to other meditation techniques.

Posture

You can sit or stand for "formal" meditation with mantras.

This is a casual way to practice. You can keep the mantra in your head, while you do other things.

Speed

Singing the mantra quickly will energize you, that is an indisputable fact. A certain rhythmic pace is helpful for calmening the mind. Your repetitions are too fast or too slow. This will cause your mind to wander and eventually fall asleep.

If you are trying to fall asleep, this is a different matter.

You will vary in the speed you repeat the mantra depending on its length: shorter mantras of one to three words are usually repeated slower than those with more syllables.

The speed of a technique can vary, so I encourage you to experiment with different repetition speeds until you find the one that works best for you.

The mantra can be recited quickly or slowly. However, if the act is done consciously it will allow the mind access to a state of silence and relief. The mantra's speed can make the silence look different.

You can recite it however you like, but it's better to keep the repetition speed constant than changing it many times during a session.

Volume and strength

If your mind is loud or irritable, you might consider "increasing the volume" of the mantra. It will make the mantra more clear and more impactful.

If your mind is quieter than usual, this is an opportunity to make the mantra more delicate. The mantra can then be recited with a low voice and in a soft, whispery voice. The mantra itself is nearly lost, and it is more perceivable as sound vibrations than a scanned phrase.

Breathing

It is difficult to adjust mantra-breath coordination. This fact is also affected by the length and meaning of the chosen word. It may be difficult to sync your mantra with breath. It is possible to inhale and breathe while pronouncing mantra. If the mantra is too short, like "om", you can repeat it twice while exhaling, and once again while inhaling. You can also speed up the pace and repeat it three time for each inhalation. Alternately, if the mantra is too long, you can inhale half of it while exhaling the second half.

Exhale. Recite the mantra during exhalation, but without making any sounds.

As an option, you may also be completely free from breathing. You can focus on the mantra and your breathing, but not on your breathing. As you practice the mantra over and over, your breathing will start to synchronize with it. It will eventually create harmony.

Mind

No matter whether you are reciting it or listening, your task is to be attentive to every single repetition. Each repetition should be fresh, new, full-of life, and fully aware.

You can make the mantra your mantra by connecting your mind with it. All of your attention should be directed at the mantra.

The mantra can be viewed as a radio station, a song of a nightingale, a flowing river or as a song. Your mind can also be a listening ear.

You'll soon realize that even if you have a thought in your head, it is a natural part of our minds to think. However, the mantra is on an even deeper and more powerful level. Your awareness should be elevated to that higher level.

Do not force your mind. Doing this would only create tension, which can be detrimental to meditation. The goal is to be mindful of the mantra for a certain time. It is a awareness that should help you relax, not force it.

The levels and the progress

Your mantra will become more powerful and more empowering if you repeat it often. Consider a mantra of one syllables. It is said that after one hundred and twenty thousand repetitions it "gets its own soul." It is our constant attention that charges the mantra. This makes the mantra your most powerful thought, and you can then count on it to bring calm and concentration into your daily life.

The mantra will get momentum and you'll find it easier to repeat. It's almost as if the mantra is lit by us, just like an incense stick. The mantra then continues on by itself, taking with it a state that induces inner peace.

This is the traditional advancement of the practice.

Verbal action: Recite it aloud. This simple trick engages the senses, making your attention more focused on your mantra.

Whispering: The lips and tongue move in a whisper, but it produces only a faint sound.

This practice is subtler and more powerful than verbal acting.

Mental acting is when you repeat the mantra in your mind only. While there may be some movement in the throat and tongue at the start, they will soon stop. The practice will then become pure mental. This stage is most common in mantra mediation.

Spontaneous hearing: You are not repeating the mantra anymore, but the mantra is still in your mind and vibrates naturally and wonderfully. There is no need for you to think about volume, speed, or anything else. You can simply listen to it, repeating it whenever you want.

As you can clearly see, there should be an incremental but noticeable progression from the initial to the final level. However, a common mistake people make when they first start to learn mantras is to jump levels and begin with mental repetitions or spontaneous repeating. Although it is possible to master mantra mediation in a conscious manner, it is much easier for beginners to start with the scale.

Did you see the shoes you can try on? It is possible that the shoe fits perfectly to our foot and we walk. However, it is not common for shoes to be truly comfortable.

Even if your preference is for verbal acting, I recommend at least a few whispered cycles of acting at the start. This will help you concentrate your mind on the mantra more easily.

Whatever your current position on this scale is, if you notice that your mind has become detached from the mantra, distracted or asleep, then stop for a while and make an effort to use it more effectively until you reach a satisfactory result.

Chapter 7: The Correct Position For The Hands In Meditation

Meditation is all about the proper position of your hands. Contrary to popular belief, you should never place your hands randomly or neglect your hands.

Each mudra stimulates various parts of the brain and assists us in channeling energy to a specific part of our body.

What does mudra really mean?

Mudra is a Sanskrit term, which literally means "seal", or "gesture", in Sanskrit. Mudras in yoga are symbolic gestures used with fingers and hands to promote energy flow and encourage meditative practices.

Below you will find nine of most common mudras and their benefits as well as instructions on how they can be performed correctly.

It is not important to keep the various names straight, instead think about how your fingers position.

Mudras are closely linked to the energy from the universe. They aim to channel it into the body for specific benefits.

Nearly every Mudra refers to a Vedic Deity. This deity in turn is associated with an aspect or energy that corresponds to a quality we wish to awaken. The mudras and divinities associated with them are connected to the five natural energies. They flow through energy channels that run right through our fingers, which reflects the psychic and spiritual levels of the body.

Each finger thus represents a point or connection to an element, and the energy associated with it. How much power do you have?

The position of the fingers can be used to control the flow and quality of the elemental energy through our bodies.

These energies are associated to every finger on the hands:

Thumb: sun, energy, fire.

Index: air and energy in motion

Medium: space, expansion, opening.

Ring finger: Earth and solidity. Rooting.

Mobility, water, and liquids:

Here's a little insight into the history of the Mudras

The practice of Mudras today is rooted in India, more than five thousand year ago. It can be found in Vedic culture as well as ancient shamanism, which suggests the use hand gestures and mantras during sacred ceremonies. The Brahmins invoked the energy from Heaven and Earth simultaneously in this ritual. It was then channeled to receive certain benefits, both material as well as spiritual.

Mudras are still used in some artistic expressions today, like the beautiful Indian dance. Here their purpose is to harmoniously support the movements of your body.

Shuni Mudra

How to run

As the thumb touches the middle fingers, the rest of your fingers will let go. For those fingers that aren't attached, you can rest your hands on your knees and relax them.

Meaning:

Shuni Mudra refers to patience. The middle finger represents perseverance and achieving your goals. While the thumb symbolises nature and the divine, the thumb symbolizes metaphorically the thumb.

These are the benefits you get

This mudra may increase or consolidate your patience. It assists us in coping with periods of change and transition, especially when we wait to reap the benefits of our labor or wait for an important result.

Surya Ravi Mudra

How to run

The thumb is slightly touched by the ring-finger, and the rest of your fingers are left relaxed. Many people recommend that you keep your fingers slightly elevated so they do not rest on your thumb.

Meaning:

This mudra is commonly known as the Sign of Life. The union of the thumb with the ring finger represents balance and good-health. The ring finger is also a symbol of perseverance and strength.

These are the benefits you get

This position can help to increase muscle strength and positive energy which can lead to optimism and constructive change.

Gyan Mudra

How to run

The thumb touches the index finger lightly and the other fingers are relaxed. This is the most common mudra used today, as it was Buddha's favorite during his meditations.

Meaning:

It is the mudra, or the gesture of knowledge. The index finger symbolises awareness, and its union with thumb represents wisdom and expansion of the ego.

These are the benefits you get

This position is meant to stimulate creativity, concentration, and alertness.

Buddhi Mudra

How to do:

The thumb touches the little finger slightly, and the other fingers remain relaxed. This mudra is more difficult than the others, as it requires more flexibility in order to keep it in place for a longer time.

Meaning:

Buddhi moudra is a position of mental clarity. The little fingers represent communication, and the union with thumb signifies openness of mind.

These are the benefits you get

This mudra balances the body's water levels. This is a great help for people with dry or sensitive mouths. It promotes communication of all kinds.

Prana Mudra

How to do:

The thumb is reached by the little finger, the ring finger, and the little finger. However the middle finger (and the index finger) remain taut.

Meaning:

This mudra is also known by the name "The position of life", because it can redirect life energy throughout the body.

These are the benefits you get

This mudra is a great way to increase energy and vitality during and after meditation. It strengthens vision, and improves immune system.

Vayu mudra

How to do:

So that pressure is exerted by the thumb, the index must be placed under it. The rest of your fingers should be kept taut. However, they shouldn't cause discomfort.

Meaning:

This mudra can be associated with air and all that is connected to it.

These are the benefits you get

This position is great for treating any air stagnation-related problems, such as flatulence or abdominal swelling.

Apaan Mudra

How to run

The thumb is touching the middle, ring and ring fingers. The little finger and forefinger stay slightly taut.

Meaning:

This mudra signifies purification.

These are the benefits you get

This position is very helpful in the elimination of toxins, especially for digestion problems.

Hakini Mudra

How to run

You can touch your fingertips with both of your hands gently but not too strongly. For the thumbs, you should apply slightly more pressure.

Meaning:

As a Hindu tradition, this mudra is used for increasing concentration and channeling energy towards third eye. This eye is found right at the forehead in the area between eyebrows.

These are the benefits you get

This position facilitates the connection of our two brain hemispheres. It promotes creativity, concentration, and memory.

Yoni Mudra

How to run

The thumb tips contact each other with moderate pressure. While the index fingers touch each others with the entire phalanx, the two index fingers touch eachother with the full first phalanx. Beginners may have difficulty understanding the position of your middle finger. Your middle fingers must touch one another perfectly. Begin by touching the second phalanx.

Meaning:

The word Yoni means "uterus" in Sanskrit. This mudra represents the isolation and abstraction from the natural world.

These are the benefits you get

This position will calm the nervous system, and help to relieve stress. It allows you complete isolation during the meditation session.

You'll soon be able to read and practice these positions until one day they are as normal as the gestures and movements you normally make every day without realizing.

Chapter 8: Transcendental Meditating: Techniques, Origins & Benefits

Hello, I'm glad we can be together again.

I hope that you are already feeling the healing effects.

We've covered several sensitive and extremely important topics and issues in the past chapters. Now it is time to look at some meditation techniques to determine which one is most appropriate for you.

Are you ready for it?

Do not be afraid, I will hold your hands.

You know well that our lives are stressful and complicated. We have to deal with the stress every day. This can be especially frustrating for some. The mind is actually a constant radio station, constantly analyzing and re-elaborating thousands of pieces of information per minute. This makes it difficult to live in harmony.

While technological and economic developments have allowed us to live in more comfortable living arrangements, they have also made it difficult to develop inner awareness and spirituality.

Transcendental Meditation was therefore designed to bridge this gap and enrich our lives.

Transcendental mediation is an easy meditation technique that beginners will love.

But what is transcendental Meditation?

Transcendental mediation is a relatively simple meditation technique. It was first developed in India and then spread by Master Maharishi throughout the 1960s.

Master Maharishi described his invention and stated that it was intended to counteract the electromagnetic waves of his thoughts, and allow the mind and the outside world to co-exist.

The transcendental Meditation also plays an important role in our personal growth. It's a meditative tool that helps us to build different religions. The recitation of the Rosary is one example of this strong practice and can be considered a mantra. From the assumption that "intending was the verb", we learn how important and powerful the word is.

Despite its anti-stress properties, it does not provide relaxation or concentration techniques. There are no rituals or positions required. It aims to reduce mental confusion from the continual passage of unnecessary and "noisy" thought. Silencing this confusion allows an individual to sharpen their personality and to be more aware of himself. This will help him live a better daily life.

It is a straightforward and natural method. You don't have to meditate for more than 20 minutes per day. Also, it doesn't affect our normal routines. This type meditation is the launch pad to a greater appreciation of the world.

This meditation technique will allow you to improve many aspects your life without requiring any effort.

It has many benefits, including reducing stress and anxiety, improving quality of sleep, increased productivity, greater clarity and productivity and lower blood pressure. Also, it can reduce stress hormone cortisol which is responsible for stress. This will also help to lower your risk of heart attack and stroke.

After earning a degree as physicist, Master Maharishi chose to spend twelve years with his master in Asia's Himalaya region, learning the basics of meditation.

His university and cultural education to that point were modern. This was a key factor in the development of his method. Maharishi first encountered meditation after he was trained by the ancient scriptures. This method is still used today.

He discovered there were originally two types, one reserved for monks or ascetics, and the other for those in a more responsible social role. The first was saved over time, but the second was lost until it almost vanished. Meditation was considered impractical and should only be practiced by monks.

Here is Master Maharishi's quote

"There are many methods to help you improve your mind. These attempts can be tedious and time-consuming. However, instead of being helpful, they can alienate from daily life, which can lead to frustration and discouragement for many. The difficulty and inefficiency of these mind-control methods is what leads to widespread belief about the difficulty and difficulties of achieving pure consciousness.

Maharishi, who was initially encouraged by his master in the first instance, decided to work hard for a solution that would make meditation more affordable to all. He found that a natural, simple and spontaneous process yielded the desired results much faster than more complicated techniques that required much more control and strength. This is how transcendental meditation was created.

Technically, the method is incredibly simple as the ultimate goal of meditation is to soothe your mind to attain pure awareness.

For 20 minutes, sit comfortably, keeping your back straight. Transcendental meditation is best practiced before meals. It is done in the morning when you wake up.

The main difference between transcendental and other forms meditation lies in how the mantra is said during the meditation session. We have discussed what mantras are in the previous chapter. The mantra helps to concentrate the mind and allows us to achieve a state of complete immobility.

Here are nine steps to help you master transcendental Meditation.

One.

Place your feet on the floor and sit down in a comfortable seat.

Retire your legs and arms to rest.

Two.

Relax your body by closing your eyes.

Three.

Then, open your eyes and close them. The practice lasts for 20 minutes. Your eyes must remain closed.

Four.

Repeat a mantra over and over in your mind. You can choose the mantra you prefer to help you relax, concentrate, and get rid of all distractions.

Five.

Recognize that your mind is being interrupted by thoughts and memories. Turn your attention back toward the mantra.

Six.

Once you feel confident in your concentration, move your focus to the height of third eye between your eyebrows.

Seven.

After twenty minutes, you can start to move your fingers to break the meditation.

Eight.

Open your eyes.

Nine.

Take a few minutes to relax before you can move on to the next part of your day.

One can transcendentally meditate by repeating a certain thought, the Mantra. It vibrates and expands in one's head until, as previously mentioned, it vibrates. Imagine the Mantra expanding to become a circular pattern on a surface of water. By doing this, the volume and frequency of thoughts will decrease until they disappear. The vibrated diffusion of the Mantra will replace them. This will allow your body and mind to rest and help you regenerate your nervous system.

Don't worry if it takes you weeks or months to master this simple exercise. I can attest to the fact that it is difficult to "turn on" your thoughts. But, once you have fully assimilated the process and continue to practice, the benefits will be unrivalled.

An open mind will lead to greater happiness and health.

A final analogy may help us to better understand Transcendental Mediation. Consider the surface of a sea. It is rough and the waves are very high. To find peace and calm, dive deep into the ocean. The lower you go, the more tranquil the sea will be until it reaches its bottom. It is possible for the sea to be both stormy at the surface and calm in its depths. If we stay at the surface, the waves can overwhelm us and cause us to be overwhelmed. However, when we go down into the depths, we can still observe the agitation.

Your mind is like a stormy river when it is constantly agitated with thoughts that chase each other. But, if your attention is focused inside, you will see that the quietness in relation increases until it reaches its peak when thoughts begin to emerge. This is the state of being completely still and content. Because transcendental meditation goes beyond any thought activity, it is also called transcendental meditation.

The inner peace found at the source is always stable and independent of anything outside. It is always there, even when we experience stress, suffering, and problems. Our well-being is affected if our awareness stays at the level the conscious mind. If the awareness of this inner peace and contentment is active throughout the day, we can face each experience without being overwhelmed, just like a shield.

Transcendental Meditation allows the conscious to spontaneously turn to its inner self, becoming aware of the deeper, quieter levels of the thought-development process. In this way, it can transcend or at least go beyond any thought impulse. It is only then that the conscious mind can remain conscious of itself. The conscious mind can become consciousness. A state of pure awareness, also known as transcendence, is when we experience an unlimited supply of energy, creativity intelligence and peace. All our thoughts are triggered by this level, which then drives all our actions.

As you become familiar with your mantra and your own awareness, your body will experience deep rest. This is designed to relieve even the most severe tensions, anxiety, stress and panic that night sleep can't eliminate. After meditation, your body will feel more rested, more vital, recharged, and will have a more creative and clearer mind. This will help you make better decisions and execute more effectively.

Summary of Transcendental Meditating.

Main features:

Recitation of mantras

Position:

sitting.

Origins:

Fifteenth-century BC, introduced in West by Maharishi Mahesh Yagi in the fifties

Benefits:

Inner harmony, tranquility, peace, awareness

Guided Meditation: 30 minute Deep Sleep Hypnosis to Improve Sleep Quality, Stress Relief, Relaxation

[To read slowly. Increase your speed to assist in bringing the more rapid state you are in of waking up into sync with the rhythmic, slower cadence of your breath and sleep.

Welcome.

After the meditation ends, it is best to experience this meditation while lying down.

(PAUSE)

Relax and let your body breathe. Allow the breath to pass through your nose. It will then travel down the length of your body, reaching your belly. As oxygenated air reaches your belly, it will rise. This is so wonderful!

When you exhale, let the things you don't use rise with your breath. You will gently breathe out through your mouth and lips, forming a small "O" shape. Exhale and feel the weight of today leave your body.

Good.

Next, take a deep breath through your nose and imagine your breath as having a color. It could be any color you choose, or even the first color you think of. This color will permeate your whole body as it travels through your nose. It will bring light, warmth, oxygen and peace. You are a body filled with this light, and infused with the newness around you. This is a system that vibrates and molecules constantly regenerating with its own wisdom. It is as simple as taking a deep breath and letting it in. Allow it to fill your life.

Wonderful.

You can exhale slowly and allow all that isn't serving you to just rise up. Notice the lightness that comes along with each breathe and let go. The peace that comes from letting go of the day. The week. What you can do without. It is easy to let them go. It's amazing how good it is to breathe in the atmosphere. To participate in the universe. To discover the grace to breathe.

Continue breathing in through the nose. Inhale light, color, and freshness into your nostrils. Next, exhale through you mouth to let out all that you have.

[1 minute silence/light music]

Beautiful.

You'll feel lighter every moment. By releasing all that doesn't serve, and accepting the expansive wisdom around you, the universe will become part of your breathing and rhythm. Just by the act of breathing. This is a way to connect with the world around you. It is so satisfying to be a part this rhythm.

Notice how your body becomes stronger and more connected to the earth. How you can be both light and part of earth. How you are in the right place at the right time, in a perfect spot in this universe.

This will allow you to find peace. Let all tension, including your mind, go into the ground. You don't have to hold on any longer. The earth has the ability to maximize the use of excess energy we don't need.

See yourself melt into the space you are in, becoming fluid, more sentient, and grace. Movement, light and movement. Breath and air. Every part of you, every cell in you body, breathes in and out the universe around them. When you stop breathing, you can see that it is actually a conversation. It is a way to connect. Breathing can be described as BEING in life.

You are the being. You are your life. You are exactly where you should be at the perfect moment. You are all you need to know right now.

Your body feels connected to the fibers beneath it. You can feel the comfort of sinking into a warm, safe place. This is where you feel secure, held and supported. You begin to sink deeper into a feeling of peace and comfort. It's simple. You simply notice how you are connected to everything around and breathe in the colors. This creates a resonance which supports you right at your current place.

When you exhale, this creates a field of color and light around you. You inhale and the color and light become part of yourself every time. When you inhale, your body feels lighter. When you exhale, your inhale deepens into the fibers below and the support of nature.

Allow your noticings and abilities to grow.

You will notice how the space around you is filled with positive light and energy. How the energies of all the universe infuse the space in which your body is located, and how that space changes. It is filled with more peace, security, comfort, love, and life.

This energy will continue to grow. You'll notice how this beautiful energy flows throughout your house and building. How your nexus is your center of breathing and imbibing energy, transforming the space around it into a more loving, peaceful and serene place. How to create a bigger sphere of radiant energy that surrounds and flows with you.

[1 minute music/silence]

Ahhhh! (sigh-like voice). This is to provoke a response in the listener. This is how the majesticity of the living environment becomes part of you. It responds to and emanates out of you. This is the magic behind breath and grounding. This is your deepest nature. It's your connected being. Being a part everything around you, helping to create what is around.

Every breath deepens your state of peace, harmony and rest.

As with a baby cradle you are held and supported. You are loved and cared for.

You begin to notice how colors shift and change, sounds soften and expand, and concrete pieces of your daily life falling away. The world blends and melds to your larger senses, with the greater consciousness of earth and with the wisdom from the whole universe. Your body relaxes and stretches, soothes and settles. You feel fluid and warm, as if you are being bathed by the universe.

Let your breath be a soothing rhythm. It will massage every cell of your body in its natural state. Massage your skull and release the tensions that are clinging to your bones, jaw, eyes, sinuses and tongue. The sweet sensation of allowing your mind to freely flow is so wonderful that your head starts to swoon. Let your head swing side-to side while you continue to unwind the neck. Release any aches, pains, stiffness, tightness, and let go of any stiffness or tightness. Fluid, light, air, oxygen, and connection to the surrounding space will occur.

Relax your shoulders into the floor below you and let go of any excess weight. As your chest relaxes in the softness your breath creates, your shoulders will drop to the surface. It is almost effortless to breathe, release, and feel a greater sense of comfort and peace. This is blissful rest.

As your abdomen becomes more softened, each and every breath will massage your belly from the inside out. Your entire body will feel the new vigor of the cells and the softness it brings. Your hips and hips are free to move in the rhythm of breathing, blood flow, and openness.

Your low back and legs follow the same pattern, rocking lightly with every inhale and then settling down until your exhale reaches your toes. Inhale any excess and exhale.

You feel lightness, watery sensations, and the stillness when you inhale. You discover that you are peace, and that this is the only way to be. It is as if you are peace.

Your body knows the best way to support you. It is able to keep your attention in deep relaxation, while remaining alert to the surrounding world. Your mind understands how to respond to the body's call for rest, to allow you to change between states, and how to listen to your body. It knows when it will be needed, but for now it is all good. There is nothing except this space, nothing except this peace, and a certainness in the wisdom that dreams.

You let yourself float and absorb the energies from the womb of your life.

Then you will drift and discover that this is a type home. An inner connection to the cosmos and everything around you. An intoxicating, flavorful connection with life that blends into your cells, with your neurons, and leads to a blissful state of serenity conducive for sleep.

Breathe, in and outside at your own pace. Allow the energies to move through and through you. Feel the expansiveness and drifting of the universe in the cells of your body and in your peaceful mind. Allow yourself time to just be.

[Music/sounds for the transition to sleep. Next 15-20minutes

[At the end, whisper this prompt]

You sink deeper into sleep when the music stops. The silence can bring you peace you have never experienced before and keep you asleep for exactly the right time.

You can breathe, and find peace in being.

You are exactly where it is you need to.

You are perfectly you.

You breathe in and out.

As the world itself breathes and unfolds.

Guided Meditation: Guided Meditation for 30 Minutes to Relax, Sleep, & Stress Relief

[Introduction- Stretching and positioning: 3 Minutes]

Before we get to the point, please take a moment to get yourself ready for a restful night.

You can prepare your room by turning off any distractions. You might need to leave your phone in another place if you feel the urge to keep checking it. Turn off the TV and any music. You want to create the right atmosphere for relaxation and rest. Dim the lights.

Place yourself on your back and lie down. You might consider putting a blanket under your knees, or a roll blanket under your head if you're uncomfortable lying on the back. Also ensure your neck, head, and neck are supported.

If you find it comfortable, move your head backward and forward. You can also turn your head sideways to loosen your neck muscles.

Let it rest in a comfortable position

Let your shoulders relax by moving them.

While your buttocks are on the bed, raise your hips and then relax your hips.

Your body should be in a neutral and comfortable place so:

Be sure your chin does not point too high. You can relax your jaw by just a little bit by pulling in slightly.

Now, you can place your shoulders beneath you. Then let your shoulders relax into a natural position.

Allow your hands to rest on your sides, palms upward or downward, or on you abdomen.

Relax your legs. If you do, your knees and feet may relax. Don't hold them in any one position; let them fall naturally.

Take a moment to give participants the opportunity to settle into a comfortable position.

[Intention setting and focusing on breathing: 10 min]

You might feel sleepy during this meditation. You may feel tired or sleepy during this meditation.

You can close your eyes and breathe easily. This is the time when you're not going to try to do anything. There's no need to fret about the future or today's events. Now, all you have to do is be there, in your body on your bed, letting the mind relax and get a good night's rest.

It is important to appreciate the self-care you have taken. You deserve to have a good night of sleep, and to wake up feeling refreshed for the day. This is the one thing you can do to yourself. There's no need to worry.

Keep in mind that you cannot fix anything that worries you or prevents you from falling asleep.

It doesn't matter how much you slept last evening or the night prior, you can still get a good night's sleep tonight. This is the night that really matters.

Give yourself a chance to think for a while

As you meditate, notice when your mind is wandering and gently tell it to return to the present moment. It's okay to let your mind wander and not judge it. This is what brains are built to do. We spend all our time trying to think of multiple things simultaneously. It can be difficult to undo years and probably not undone today. However, you have already started to do the best you can to unclutter your brain.

Breathe in and out naturally for a few seconds.

You can think about your breathing, but you should not change it. This is your natural and healthy breath. This is what you do every day. Concentrate on this activity for just a few short minutes. It's easy and takes very little effort.

Give yourself a moment of reflection

Take a few deep inhalations and let go of any tension. You can feel the air's movement by slowing down your inhale. It is normal to be able to breath less than you can. At this moment, it is normal to want to inhale as deeply as possible.

Take a deep inhale. Allow the air to flow through your nostrils into your lungs, and then into your abdomen. You should breathe in as deeply and as long as you can.

Slowly exhale. Push the air out from your abdomen, then your lungs.

Now think about the tightness in your chest that you may have felt while you were taking that last breath. Consider how it feels to be able to relax any areas that feel stuck.

Next, you will take a few deep breathes again. Now, relax into the breath. While I will give you some guidelines for relaxation, don't feel pressure to keep up with my pace. Simply keep your breathing deep and use the instructions for each breath.

You shouldn't force the air out of your stomach when you exhale. Relax and let the exhale flow naturally.

When you take a deep breath, notice the flow of air through your nostrils. When deep breathing becomes difficult, some people tighten the throat. To open your throat and allow air to flow freely through it, try to tucking your chin just a bit.

Take a slow inhale, allowing the air to escape your body.

Give yourself a minute to think.

You can inhale deep again and feel the air moving through your throat and nostrils into your lungs. Relax your chest, and allow your lungs to expand with each inhale. You should think about your lungs expanding outwards and not upwards. If your shoulders feel raised, try to relax them while your lungs expand.

You can exhale fully again. You can inhale deeply, relax your shoulder and move your lungs to the side.

Take a deep breath and exhale.

Give yourself a minute to think.

When you inhale deeply, feel the air flow through your nostrils and down your throat into your lungs. You will feel your abdomen rising as you fill your lungs. Relax your stomach and let it out. Do not worry, no one is looking. You can use your stomach to fill your lungs fuller. Most people aren't comfortable relaxing their stomachs in this way. We don't want it to be pushed out or look fat. However, know that no one will be watching you right now.

You can exhale naturally. Relax your stomach and repeat the process. Feel the air moving out of your abdomen and inhale deeply. Relax your shoulders and let your stomach push forward.

Do three more deep breathing exercises at your own pace. Then, check for any tension. These areas can be addressed without judgment. You don't have to worry if you feel them tight. Keep an eye out for them when you shift your focus elsewhere.

Relax your mind and allow yourself to feel at peace.

Give yourself a minute to think.

[Bodyscan: 10 minutes]

As your body relaxes, you may feel it becoming heavier. See how your body rests on the ground. You are supported by the objects around you as you meditate. They will hold you steady and enable you to do the work necessary to clear your mind.

Your body could hold tension, similar to your breath. We can release these tensions and relax our bodies by scanning them. If you feel tension in your body, relax these muscles. The tension may be reduced by a simple stretch or release of muscles. This does not have to be a large movement. It resets muscle memory to a state of relaxation and not tension.

Your attention should be at the top of you head. Imagine how that feeling feels. You might feel the breeze or warmth. It may be difficult to feel your top of the head if it isn't thought about. You can imagine it touching the air. You might feel heat or a breeze. It doesn't matter how strong or weak you feel.

Give yourself a minute to think.

Focus your attention on your cheeks and around the mouth.. Notice where tension is held. What would it feel like to release tension? Your lips should be lowered and you can smile softly. This smile is mostly internal. Smiles are good for your face and can help you relax. Do not worry if you find it funny. Relax and let it happen.

Give yourself a minute to think.

Now focus your attention on your neck and shoulders. These are common areas where stress and tension can be stored. These areas can become very restrictive and you might not be able imagine how it would feel to relax. Try stretching your shoulders and tucking the chin. Move your head around a bit. If you experience pain from any of these actions, stop. Let your shoulders feel heavy, and your neck relax. Be open to feeling what your neck and shoulders feel like. No matter how much you relax them, they will feel more relaxed than ever before.

Give yourself a minute to think.

Pay attention to your abdomen, stomach and heart. Notice if there is tension in those areas. Nerves and worries love to settle in those areas. These can be let go of for now. They will be back if you need them. For a limited time, however, you can let those go. Maybe your worries have made you think about what you need to do. You already know that you will get to these things when you finish this. While you wait, prepare your mind. You won't be able to help them if your stomach is full. It's important to keep your stomach and chest open so that you can focus on the things you really want.

Give yourself a minute to think.

Focus your attention on your arms. While they may feel heavy to your eyes, this is normal. Give them a chance to relax however much you find comfortable. You can notice if there is tension in your hands. If so, you can stretch your fingers to let it go. Allow them to relax, and then rest your feet on the floor or your legs.

Give yourself a minute to think.

Focus your attention on your pelvis, lower back and pelvis. It may be that you have been sitting still for several minutes. Allow your lower back to relax and allow you to move a little. Pay close attention to the areas where tension is present in your pelvis. Don't let any tension hold you back.

Give yourself a chance to think for a while

Now focus on your legs and feet. Sometimes our legs are so strong that we don't notice the tension in the thighs. You can let the falls happen naturally and keep your feet connected with the floor. If you're lying down, let the feet and knees fall naturally to one side. To relax, you might try stretching or wiggling your feet.

Take three deep breaths at a pace that suits you. You can linger on the exhale, but not forcefully.

Feel the sensation of total relaxation. This is the first time you've felt this relaxed in quite some time. It's possible to achieve this level of relaxation at any time.

Refrain from thinking for a second

[Conclusion: 7 minutes]

Keep your attention on your breath. Your breathing should be natural. Notice the inhale, exhale. You don't have to force it. Notice when you are breathing faster or slower than normal and allow the urge to control it to go. Normaly, you don't think about your breathing. People often notice the difference in their breathing and begin to pay more attention.

This is a light focus of your breath.

It's just .... And .....

One breath, ... Out

Notice when your mind wanders. Take a few deep breaths to catch your attention and bring it back to you.

Just this breath .....

Take each breath one by one.

You can take a break for a few moments of silence.

Thank yourself for taking the effort to prepare yourself for sleep and settle your mind. Although it may not feel like it but this is an important step towards relaxation and clearing your mind. This will help to let go of any thoughts or worries that may prevent you from falling asleep well.

It is possible to achieve this level every night before bed. If you desire this, take a moment just to breathe and remind yourself that tension and worries are distractions that can be put aside so you can focus on the important things. Keep your eyes on the breath and let them go if they start to creep into your thoughts.

Inhale

Breathe

Take a deep inhale and feel your body sink into the mattress. This is rest. This is how we replenish.

Allow yourself to feel it fully and completely.

Allow yourself to rest.

Guided Meditation for Better Sleep: One hour of deep sleep hypnosis and music for daily stress relief, relaxation and to reduce anxiety.

Notes for the speaker are in brackets and in italics. This text should not be read fast. Allow plenty of time for words to sink into your brain and for you to drift off to sleep. In the text, there are several pauses. The transition between focusing on the physical and becoming aware of a subtler, more spiritual body will draw the listener in.

Welcome.

The guided meditation you are about to start will help you relieve stress and tension so you can get into deep sleep. Before we begin, please be comfortable. When you're done with the meditation, you should lie down in a warm, comfortable place. To begin, bring awareness fully to the body. After that, you'll be able to relax and drift into deep, comfortable sleep.

These thirty minutes will be yours. This is your opportunity. You don't even have to do it.

Let the rest and the days that have passed since then drift away. Everything you've done and everything you've felt today; the conversations you had with the people that you've met - all of that begins to fade. Imagine yourself walking in this room, closing your eyes and lying down.

Be aware that you are entitled to this time. Listening to this recording is a way to show yourself and your body love. You will also be able to give love and care to others by doing so.

Now, take a deep breathe in through your nose and exhale through you mouth.

Continue to inhale deep through your mouth and then exhale through you nose.

Let's go again.

Rest your right hand on the lower part of your abdomen. Now, move your left arm towards your chest. Now take a deep breath in to your right-hand, and fill your belly as high as you can. Inhale into your right-hand, so your belly sinks.

Repeat the above: Exhale right. Now exhale right. Three more times. Take a deep breath. Your belly will rise. To lower your belly, exhale right. Inhale right hand, belly falls. Inhale right hand, exhale right hand. Inhale, exhale.

Next, inhale slowly into the left side. Deep inhale. Fill your whole chest with the breathe. You can exhale using your left hand. Take a deep breath and exhale. Three more times. Breathe left. Inhale until your chest reaches the collar bone. Exhale. Exhale left and inhale right. Inhale, exhale.

Then, we'll connect them. Next, exhale deeply in the right hand. This will cause the belly to rise and the left hand to raise the chest. Exhale left-hand - chest falls. Inhale right-hand - belly falls. Inhale right, left. Inhale left, right. Ten more times like this. Deep, complete breaths

[Pause. Allow 40 seconds to take deep, calming breaths or listen to music.

That's great.

Now let go.

Pay attention to the sensations of your breath in the body. You can take a few minutes to look at the rhythm of your breathe and see where it goes. Do not try to control the breath - there is no right or wrong. It's okay to observe the breath patterns and the depth of each one without judgment.

[Allow at least one minute for unguided breath here]

Continue to breathe with a calm, uncontrolled, unhurried pace. Your body knows how this works.

Your body knows how you can support yourself throughout the day, night, and when to take a deep breath and how quickly. Your body is supported by your muscles, bones and organs. Your body knows how to get you to sleep. Be open to the wisdom of your body as you feel your eyelids getting heavier. There is no problem to solve, and nothing to discover.

You'll feel refreshed after you wake up from this sleep. You will feel refreshed and like you've actually slept. Your skin will feel more radiant. You will have clearer thinking. You will feel more patient and better equipped for dealing with daily challenges. Your body will be more resilient. Your body will be more resilient after you have given it time to heal from the daily stresses of being overweight and the demands of living. Your digestive system will have had time for rest and recovery, to replenish nutrients and remove toxins. Your brain will have processed your thoughts and organised them so that you can manage the worries of today.

This type of sleep can bring clarity and strength.

Pay attention now to your spine. Pay attention to what happens when your breath enters or leaves your body. As you focus on the spine, you will notice that it lengthens with every inhale. This subtle change may not be obvious, but it is worth paying attention for a moment. As you breathe in, your spine will lengthen. As the breath comes in, the spine lengthens.

Take a few deep, slow breaths. Notice the subtle, natural movement in your spine. The spine is always connected to the breath. The spine and the breath support you always.

[Pause, 30 seconds]

Good.

There are 24 articulated vertebrae within the spine. Bring your attention to the lumbar vertebra - at the base of the spine. From here, move your awareness slowly up the spine, one vertebra each. As you hear me mention each vertebra, visualize the space between them growing larger. Allow the spine to relax fully.

You should start at the base, in your lumbar spine.

One.

Two.

Three.

Four.

Five.

We now move on to the middle section, or thoracic spine.

Six.

Seven.

Eight.

Nine.

Ten.

Eleven.

Twelve.

Thirteen.

Fourteen.

Fifteen.

Sixteen.

Seventeen.

The top of the spine is then the cervical spine.

Eighteen.

Nineteen.

Twenty.

Twenty-one.

Twenty-two.

Twenty-three.

Twenty-four.

Bring awareness to the length of the spine.

The spine has a long length. The spine is relaxed. Relaxed back. The breath flows naturally, gently.

www.ingramcontent.com/pod-product-compliance
Lightning Source LLC
Chambersburg PA
CBHW050403120526
44590CB00015B/1812